HOLY VEDAS

Swami Divyananda

Published by

GRAPEVINE INDIA PUBLISHERS PVT LTD

www.grapevineindia.com
Delhi | Mumbai
email: grapevineindiapublishers@gmail.com

Ordering Information:
Quantity sales: Special discounts are available on quantity purchases by corporations, associations, and others. For details, reach out to the publisher.

First published by Grapevine India 2019

Printed at Nutech Print Services - India

CONTENTS

ॐ भूर्भुवः स्वः

तत्सवितुर्वरेण्यं

भर्गो देवस्य धीमहि

धीयो यो नः प्रचोदयात् ।।

RIG VEDA

CREATION - HYMNS

Non-being then existed not nor being:
There was no air, nor sky that is beyond it.
What was concealed? Wherein? In whose protection?
And was there deep unfathomable water?

Death then existed not nor life immortal;
Of neither night nor day was any token.
By its inherent force the One breathed windless:
No other thing than that beyond existed.

Darkness there was at first by darkness hidden;
Without distinctive marks, this all was water.
That which, becoming, by the void was covered,
That One by force of heat came into being.

VARUNA

The greatest of the gods of the Rigveda, beside Indra, is Varuna, though the number of hymns in which he alone (apart from Mitra) is addressed is only 12, as compared with the 250 to Indra. His physical features and activities are mentioned: he has face, eye, arms, hands and feet; he walks, drives, sits, eats and drinks. His eye, with which he observes mankind, is the sun.

He sits on the strewn grass at the sacrifice. He wears a golden mantle or a shining robe. His car, drawn by well-yoked steeds, gleams like the sun. Varuna sits in his mansion surveying the deeds of men; and the Fathers behold him in the highest heaven. He has spies who sit around him and observe the two worlds. By his golden - winged messenger the sun is meant. He is often called a king, but especially a universal monarch.

His sovereignty, his divine dominion, and his occult power (mayo) are specially emphasized. Varuna is characteristically an upholder of physical and moral order, the great maintainer of the laws of nature. He established heaven and earth, which he keeps asunder.

VARUNA - HYMNS

Present to Varuna the gracious giver
A hymn, Vasistha, bright and very pleasant,
That he may bring to us the lofty, holy
And mighty steed that grants a thousand bounties.

Now having come to Varuna's full aspect,
I think his countenance like that of Agni;
May he, the lord, lead me to see the marvel:
The light and darkness hidden in the cavern.

When Varuna and I the boat have mounted
And have propelled it to the midst of ocean;
When we shall move across the waters' ridges
We'll waver in the swing to raise its lustre.

MITRA

Mitra is so intimately associated with Varuna that he is invoked alone in only one hymn of the Rigveda. The information about him in his separate capacity being so limited, his individual character is somewhat indefinite. He is the great Aditya who by his voice marshals men and watches the tillers with unwinking eye.

That he is thought of as regulating the course of the sun is indicated by the fact that the solar deity Savitar is identified with him because of his laws, and another solar deity, Visnu, takes his three strides by the laws of Mitra. Agni, who is kindled before dawn, is said to produce Mitra, and when kindled is identified with Mitra. In the Atharvaveda Mitra at sunrise is contrasted with Varuna in the evening, and in the Brahmanas Mitra is associated with day, Varuna with night.

The Vedic evidence thus indicates that Mitra is a solar deity. This conclusion is confirmed by the cognate Iranian religion, in which Mithra is undoubtedly a sun-god.

MITRA HYMNS

Mitra stirs men to action when he calls them;
Mitra supported both the Earth and Heaven;
Mitra with steady eye regards the people:
To Mitra offer now with ghee oblation.

Let him who, Mitra L brings thee food be foremost,
Who to thy law, O Aditya, pays homage.
Aided by thee no man is slain or vanquished;
To him from near or far no trouble reaches.

Free from disease, in sacred food delighting,
With knees set firm upon the earth's wide surface.
In this Aditya's sacred law abiding,
May we remain in the good will of Mitra.

MITRA & VARUNA

These two gods are addressed as a pair in the dual more frequently than any other couple except Heaven and Earth. The hymns in which they are thus conjointly invoked are far more numerous than those in which they are separately addressed.

As Mitra by himself has hardly any individual traits, the two gods together have practically the same attributes and functions as Varuna alone.

Mitra-Varuna are young and wear glistening garments. Their eye is the sun; they drive with the rays of the sun as with arms. They mount their car in the highest heaven. Their abode, which is golden, is located in heaven; it is great, very lofty, firm, with a thousand pillars and a thousand doors. They have spies who are wise and cannot be deceived. They are kings and universal monarchs, rulers and guardians of the whole world, who support heaven, air and earth.

MITRA & VARUNA - HYMNS

The beauteous eye of Varuna and Mitra,
The Sun, now rises up, his light extending,
Who with his gaze looks down upon all creatures:
He ever notes the burning zeal of mortals.

This pious priest, heard far away, here utters
His hymn for you, O Varuna and Mitra:
Do ye, O sages, treat his prayers with favour,
And may his autumns be replete with wisdom.

From wide-spread earth, O Varuna and Mitra,
Ye bounteous gods, and from the lofty heaven,
Ye have disposed your wander ing spies in dwellings
And plants, ye who with watchful eye protect us.

THE ADITYAS

The group of gods called Adityas is celebrated in six entire hymns of the Rigveda and in parts of two others. Their original number was seven, but in one passage of the last book, an eighth, Martanda (probably the setting sun) is added. In the Atharvaveda their number is eight. In the Brahmanas it has grown to twelve; and in post-Vedic literature these are regularly twelve sun-gods connected with the twelve months.

The names of the gods included in this group are not quite definite. Nowhere are more than six enumerated, and that only once: Mitra, Aryaman, Bhaga, Varuna, Daksa, Amsa. In a few passages Surya is called an Aditya, which is a common name of the sun in the Brahmanas and later. He is therefore probably to be regarded as the seventh Aditya. Indra is, however, once coupled in the dual as an Aditya with Varuna, the chief of the Adityas, and he is once directly invoked as the "fourth Aditya."

THE ADITYAS - HYMNS

These songs that drip with butter, with the ladle
I ever to the kings, Adityas, offer.
May Mitra, Aryaman, and Bhaga hear us,
Daksa, the mighty Varuna, and Amsa.

This praise of mine may Aryaman and Mitra
And Varuna to-day accept united:
The radiant Adityas, like sword-blades shining,
From guile and falsehood free, unscathed, and blameless.

These Adityas are deep and far-extending,
With many eyes, deceived not, but deceiving.
They look within, and see the straight and crooked.
Nigh to the kings is all, even what is farthest.

SURYA

Surya, who is addressed in about ten hymns of the Rigveda,) is the most concrete of the solar deities, because his name designates the orb of the sun as well as the god.

The solar disc is often called the eye of Surya, or the eye of Mitra-Varuna, as well as of Agni and of the gods. He is all-seeing, the spy of the whole world, beholding the good and bad deeds of mortals. His car is drawn by a single steed or by seven swift mares. The Dawn reveals or produces Surya; like a lover he follows the radiant goddess. He arouses men to activity; he is the soul of all that moves or stands.

He is the son of Heaven (Dyaus). Surya is variously described as a bird traversing space; as a mottled bull or a brilliant steed; as a gem of the sky, or a variegated stone set in the midst of heaven; as a brilliant weapon ; or as a wheel, though the wheel of Surya is also spoken of. He dispels the darkness, which he casts off like a skin. He measures the days and prolongs life. He drives away disease and evil dreams.

SURYA - HYMNS

The gods' refulgent countenance has risen,
The eye of Mitra, Varuna and Agni.
He has pervaded air, and earth, and heaven:
The soul of all that moves and stands is Surya.

The Sun pursues the Dawn, the gleaming goddess,
As a young man a maiden, to the region
Where god-devoted men lay on the harness
Of brilliant offerings for the brilliant godhead.

The brilliant steeds, bay coursers of the sun-god,
Refulgent, dappled, meet for joyful praises,
Wafting our worship, heaven's ridge have mounted,
And in one day round earth and sky they travel.

PUSAN

This god, who is celebrated in eight hymns, has a vague personality, with few anthropomorphic traits. His foot, his right hand, his beard and his braided hair are mentioned. He carries a golden spear, an awl and a goad. His car is drawn by goats instead of horses. Gruel is his characteristic food. He sees all creatures clearly. He moves onward, observing the universe, and makes his abode in heaven.

He is a guardian who knows and surveys all creatures. He traverses the distant path of heaven and earth. With his golden aerial ships he acts as the messenger of Surya.

As best of charioteers he drove down the golden wheel of the sun. He is the wooer of his mother and the lover of his sister (i.e. Dawn), and was given by the gods as a husband to the Sun-maiden, Surya. One of his exclusive epithets is "glowing." He conducts the dead on the far-off path of the Fathers. A guardian of roads, he removes dangers out of the way.

PUSAN - HYMNS

O Pusan pass along the roads,
Free us, son of release, from care.
Guide us, going before, god,

The wicked, ill-intentioned wolf,
Pusan, that lies in wait for us,
Him from our path smite thou away.

The robber lurking round our path,
Who there against us mischief plots,
Far from the track drive him away.

Tread under foot the burning brand
Of crafty and malignant men,
The miscreants whoe'er they be.

SAVITAR

Savitar is invoked in eleven whole hymns and in a good many detached stanzas as well. He is pre-eminently a golden deity. His golden car is drawn by two or more brown, white-footed steeds.

With his golden arms, which he raises aloft, he arouses and blesses all beings. His mighty golden splendour illumines heaven, earth and air. He moves in his golden car on an upward and a downward path, observing all creatures. Yellow-haired, he constantly raises his light in the east.

On his ancient paths in the air he conveys the dead to where the righteous dwell, He drives away evil dreams and sins, demons and sorcerers.

He observes fixed laws. Wind and waters are subject to, and regulated by him. He brings not only day but night, when he sends all beings to rest. The other gods follow his lead, and no being can resist his will.

SAVITAR - HYMNS

God Savitar, the dexterous, has stretched aloft
His arms, that he may stimulate all things to life.
Young, vigorous, most skilled, with fatness he
His hands besprinkles in the wide expanse of air.

May we possess god Savitar's most excellent
Impulsion, and enjoy his lavish gifts of wealth.
Thou art the god who sends to rest and wakes in turn
To life the whole two-footed and four-footed world.

With guards that never fail, auspicious, Savitar,
Protect our habitation all around to-day.
God of the golden tongue, for welfare ever new
Preserve us: let no plotter hold us in his grasp.

VISNU

Visnu, though one of the two leading gods of modern Hinduism, is in the Rigveda as yet a minor deity, being addressed in only five or six hymns.

The only anthropomorphic traits there attributed to him are that he is a youth of vast body and that he takes three strides. The latter is his chief characteristic, with which are associated his exclusive epithets of "wide-going" and "wide-striding." With these steps he traverses the earth and the terrestrial regions.

Two of his steps are visible to men, but the third is beyond the flight of birds or mortal ken. His highest step is like an eye fixed in heaven; it shines down brightly. Visnu's three strides undoubtedly refer to the course of the sun as it passes through the three divisions of the world: earth, air and heaven.

Visnu is further said to set in motion his 90 steeds (i.e. days) with their four names (i.e. seasons), in allusion to the 360 days of the solar year. Thus Visnu seems to have been originally a personification of the sun in its activity of traversing the universe.

VISNU - HYMNS

I will proclaim the mighty deeds of Visnu,
Of him who measured out the earthly spaces:
Who, firmly propping up the higher station,
Strode out in triple regions, widely pacing.

Because of this his mighty deed is Visnu
Lauded, like some fierce beast that is much dreaded,
That wanders as it lists, that haunts the mountains:
He in whose three wide strides abide all creatures.

Let my inspiring hymn go forth to Visnu,
The mountain-dwelling bull, the widely pacing,
Him who has measured out with but three footsteps,
Alone, this long and far-extended station.

USAS

Usas, the goddess of Dawn, who is celebrated in some twenty hymns of the Rigveda, is but slightly personified, for the underlying physical phenomenon is never absent from the mind of the poet.

She appears in the east, clothed in light, adorned with bright raiment like a dancer. She drives away the darkness and removes the black robe of night. Though ancient, she is ever young, being born again and again. She wastes away the life of mortals.

She opens the gates of heaven, and her radiant beams appear like herds of cattle. She rides on a brilliant car, drawn by ruddy steeds or kine. She drives away bad dreams, evil spirits and the hateful darkness. When she shines forth, the birds fly from their nests, and men seek nourishment.

She appears day after day at the appointed place, never infringing the law of nature and of the gods. She is born in the sky, and is constantly called the "daughter of heaven."

USAS - HYMNS

She throws gay garments round her like a dancing girl;
E'en as a cow her udder, she displays her breast.
Creating light for all the world, Dawn has unbarred
The gates of darkness as when cows break from their stall.

Her radiant shimmer has appeared before us;
It spreads, and drives away the swarthy monster.
As one anoints the post at sacrifices
The daughter of the sky extends her lustre.

We have crossed to the farther shore of darkness:
Dawn shining forth, her webs of light is weaving.
She smiles for glory, radiant, like a lover.
To show good will she, fair of face, has wakened.

RATRI

The following is the only hymn of the Rigveda in which, under the name of Ratri, the goddess of night is invoked. Like her sister, Usas, she is a daughter of Heaven. She is conceived not as the dark, but as the bright, starlit night, shining with her eyes.

Decked with all splendour, she drives away the darkness. At her approach, men, beasts and birds go to rest. Protecting her worshippers from the wolf and the thief, she guides them to safety. Under the name of nakta combined with ufas, Night appears as a dual divinity with Dawn in some twenty scattered stanzas of the Rigveda.

RATRI - HYMNS

When night comes on, the goddess shines
In many places with her eyes:
All glorious she has decked herself.

Immortal goddess far and wide,
She fills the valleys and the heights:
Darkness she drives away with light.

The goddess now, as she comes on,
Is turning out her sister, Dawn:
Far off the darkness hastes away.

So, goddess, come to-day to us:
At thy approach we seek our homes,
As birds their nests upon the tree.

THE ASVINS

Next to Indra, Agni and Soma, the twin deities, called Asvins, "Horsemen," are the most prominent gods in the Rigveda, being invoked in more than 50 entire hymns and in parts of several others. The time of their appearance is between dawn and sunrise, when darkness still abides among the ruddy cows (i.e. the rays of dawn). Usas awakens them; she is followed by them on their car. They dispel darkness and drive away evil spirits. Their car, which was fashioned by the three divine artificers, the Rbhus, and is sunlike and golden, is threefold and has three wheels. It is drawn by horses, or by birds, or by winged steeds. Its revolving course traverses heaven and earth in one day.

The Asvins are the children of Heaven, but are once called the sons of Vivasvant (the sun) and Saranyu (probably the dawn). Pusan is once said to be their son, and Dawn is probably meant by their sister. They are often associated with the daughter of the sun, Surya, who rides with them on their car and is their spouse.

THE ASVINS - HYMNS

Night hastens far away from Dawn, her sister;
The Black one yields the ruddy god a pathway.
We call on you two rich in kine and horses:
By day and night ward off from us the arrow.

Come to the pious mortal bringing bounty,
O Asvins, hither with your chariot speeding.
Do ye ward off from us disease and weakness.
By day and night, lovers of sweetness, guard us.

May your propitious coursers whirl your chariot
Toward us at the dawn now flushing on us.
Bring it, by traces drawn and fraught with riches,
Hither with horses yoked by Order, Asvins.

INDRA

Indra, being the favourite national god of the Vedic people, is invoked in about one-fourth of the hymns of the Rigveda in far more than are addressed to any other deity. He is more anthropomorphic and more invested with mythological imagery than any other Vedic god.

He is primarily a deity of the thunderstorm, who vanquishes the demons of drought or darkness, setting free the waters or winning the light. His physical parts, such as his body and his head, are often mentioned. His form, as well as his hair and his beard, is tawny.

His two arms are especially often referred to as wielding the thunderbolt (vafra), which is his exclusive weapon. This missile, fashioned for him by the artificer god, Tvastar, is made of iron, but sometimes of stone, is sharp and many-pointed, and golden or tawny in colour. Sometimes he is armed with bow and arrows, and he also carries a hook. His golden car is drawn by two tawny steeds.

Indra is, more than any other god, addicted to Soma, which stimulates him to carry out his warlike deeds, especially the slaughter of the demon Vrtra.

INDRA - HYMNS

I will proclaim the manly deeds of Indra,
The first that he performed, the lightning-wielder.
He slew the serpent, then discharged the waters,
And cleft the caverns of the lofty mountains.

He slew the serpent lying on the mountain:
For him the whizzing bolt has Tvastar fashioned.
Like lowing cows, with rapid current flowing,
The waters to the ocean down have glided.

Impetuous like a bull he chose the Soma,
And drank in threefold vessels of its juices.
The bounteous god grasped lightning for his missile;
He struck down dead that first-born of the serpents.

PARJANYA

Parjanya is a subordinate deity in the Rigveda, being invoked in three hymns only. He is a rain-god. The name often means "rain-cloud," but generally represents its personification.

It is often alluded to as an udder, a pail, or a water-skin. Parjanya is frequently spoken of as a bull that quickens the plants and the earth.

The shedding of rain is his most prominent characteristic: he flies around with a watery car and loosens the water-skin, shedding rain-water as our divine father; he is then associated with thunder and lightning. He is in a special degree a nourisher of vegetation, and also a producer of animal fertility. He is several times called a father. He is once said to be the son of heaven, and his wife is by implication the earth.

PARJANYA - HYMNS

Invoke the mighty god with songs of welcome;
Parjanya praise: with homage seek to win him.
He, roaring like a bull, with streams that quicken,
A seed to germinate in plants deposits.

The trees he shatters and he smites the demon host:
The whole world trembles at his mighty weapon's stroke,
The guiltless man himself flees from the potent god,
When miscreants Parjanya with his thunder strikes.

Like charioteer his horses lashing with a whip,
The god makes manifest his messengers of rain. .
From far away the roaring of the lion sounds,
What time Parjanya veils the firmament with rain.

RUDRA

Rudra is invoked alone in only three entire hymns. His hand, his arms, and his limbs are mentioned, and he is described as having beautiful lips and braided hair. He is brown in colour and shines like the radiant sun, being arrayed in golden ornaments and wearing a glorious necklace. He drives in a car; he holds the thunderbolt in his arm, and discharges his lightning shaft from the sky; but he is usually armed with a bow and arrows.

Rudra is often associated with the Maruts, whose father he is. He is fierce and destructive like a terrible beast, being called a bull and the ruddy boar of heaven.

He is unsurpassed in might, young and unaging, a lord and father of the world. By his rule and universal dominion he is aware of the doings of men and gods.

He is bountiful, easily invoked and auspicious. But he is usually malevolent; for the hymns addressed to him chiefly express fear of his terrible shafts and deprecation of his wrath.

RUDRA - HYMNS

Let thy goodwill, O father of the Maruts,
Light on us: part us not from Surya's vision.
In mercy may the hero spare our horses:
May we, O Rudra, have abundant offspring.

By thy most wholesome remedies, O Rudra,
Thy gifts, I would attain a hundred autumns.
Drive far away from us distress and hatred,
Drive far away, wide-scattered, all diseases.

Of what is born thou art the chief in glory,
Armed with the thunder, mightiest of the mighty.
Transport us to the farther shore of trouble
In safety; frustrate all attacks of mischief.

MARUTS

The Maruts, or Storm-gods, are prominent deities in the Rigveda, being invoked in 33 hymns alone, and in 9 others in association with other gods (Indra, Agni, Pusan). They form a group, being mentioned in the plural only. Their number is stated as thrice seven or thrice sixty. They are the sons of Rudra and Prsni (who probably represents the mottled storm-cloud).

But they are also said to have been generated by Vayu, god of wind, or to be the sons of heaven, or even to be self-born. They are brothers of equal age, having the same birthplace and abode. The goddess Rodasi is always connected with them as riding on their car.

She seems to have been regarded as their bride.

The brilliance of the Maruts is characteristic, and they are very frequently associated with lightning. They have spears of lightning and wear golden helmets. They are armed with golden axes, but sometimes with bows and arrows, like their father Rudra.

MARUTS - HYMNS

When, Maruts, now for you the sage
Pours out the threefold Soma draught,
Ye shine forth on the mountain heights.

Whenever, bright ones, growing strong,
You have decided on your course,
The mountains bend and bow themselves.

Loud roaring with the winds, the sons
Of Prsni raise themselves aloft:
They have milked out the swelling draught.

The Maruts scatter mist abroad,
They make the mountain ridges quake,
When with the winds they go their way.

VATA

The god of Wind is invoked by the two names of Vayu and Vata, both derived from the root va, "to blow." The former is addressed in one whole hymn and parts of others, the latter in two short hymns. Both names are sometimes used in the same verse, but Vayu is more often the god, Vata the element. In keeping with the latter distinction, Vayu is often associated with the anthropomorphic Indra as a dual divinity, while Vata is similarly coupled with Parjanya, whose connexion with the thunderstorm is more vivid and realistic than that of Indra. Different sets of epithets are applied to these two wind-gods. Vayu has a shining car drawn by a team or by a pair of ruddy steeds. He is fond of Soma, and is its protector. He grants fame, offspring and wealth; he disperses foes and protects the weak. Vata is the breath of the gods; like Rudra he wafts healing and prolongs life, for he has the treasure of immortality in his house.

He is chiefly mentioned in connexion with the thunderstorm, and his noise is often referred to. He produces ruddy lights and makes the dawns to shine. His swiftness often supplies a comparison for the speed of the gods or of mythical steeds.

VATA - HYMNS

Of Vata's car I now will praise the greatness:
Rending it speeds along; its noise is thunder.
Touching the sky it flies, creating lightnings;
Scattering dust it traverses earth's ridges.

The hosts of Vata onward speed together:
They haste to him as women to a concourse.
The god with them upon the same car mounted,
The king of all this universe speeds onward.

In air, along his pathways speeding onward,
Never on any day he tarries resting.
The first-born order-loving friend of waters:
Where was he born, and whence has he arisen?

APAS: WATERS

The waters, which are invoked in four entire hymns, as well as in a few detached stanzas, are personified only to the extent of being thought of as mothers, young wives and goddesses, bestowing boons and coming to the sacrifice. They follow the path of the gods.

They flow in a channel dug out with his bolt by Indra, whose ordinances they never infringe. The sea is their goal. But they are also celestial; for their abode is with the gods, in the seat of Mitra-Varuna, beside the sun. King Varuna moves in their midst, looking down on the truth and falsehood of men. As mothers they produce not only Agni, but all that is fixed or moves. They purify and carry away defilement.

They also cleanse from moral guilt from the sins of violence, cursing and lying. They further bestow remedies, health, strength, long life, wealth and immortality. Their favour is often invoked, and they are invited to receive the Soma libation, seated on the sacrificial grass.

The waters are often associated with honey: their milk mixed with honey is produced in the sky, gladdens the gods, and became the drink of Indra, giving him heroic strength.

APAS: WATERS - HYMNS

With ocean for their chief they flow unresting;
From the aerial flood they hasten cleansing;
For whom the mighty Indra's bolt cut channels,
Here may those waters, goddesses, preserve me.

Waters that come from heaven or run in channels
Dug out, or flow spontaneously by nature,
That, clear and pure, have as their goal the ocean;
Here may those waters, goddesses, preserve me.

In midst of whom king Varuna is moving,
And looking down surveys men's truth and falsehood:
Who, clear and purifying, drip with sweetness:
Here may those waters, goddesses, preserve me.

APAM NAPAT

Apam Napat, the Son of Waters, is invoked in one entire hymn and is often incidentally mentioned elsewhere. He is youthful and brilliant, shining without fuel in the waters that surround and nourish him. Clothed with lightning he is of golden aspect, shining with undimmed splendour in the highest place. He is borne by steeds swift as thought. In the last stanza of the following hymn he is invoked as Agni, who, moreover, is called Apam Napat in an Agni hymn; the epithet, "swiftly-speeding," is further applied to these two deities exclusively, though they are otherwise sometimes distinguished.

Apam Napat thus appears to represent the lightning form of Agni hidden in the cloud. For Agni is not only directly called Apam Napat, but also described as the "embryo of the waters"; the third form of Agni is, moreover, said to be kindled in the waters.

This god is an inheritance from pre-Indian mythology, for in the Avesta Apam Napat is a spirit of the waters who lives in their depths, surrounded by females and often invoked with them, who drives with swift steeds, and is associated with brilliance in the depth of the ocean.

APAM NAPAT - HYMNS

Desiring gain this eloquence I utter:
May the streams' son accept my songs with gladness.
Will he, the Son of Waters, of swift impulse,
Perchance reward them well? He will enjoy them.

Now from our hearts we would this hymn well-fashioned
Address to him: perchance he will regard it.
The noble Son of Waters, by the greatness
Of rule divine, all creatures has created.

Some flow together, some approach the ocean;
The rivers thus fill up the common cistern.
And him the pure, the shining Son of Waters,
The waters pure on all sides have surrounded.

PRTHIVI: EARTH

The following hymn is the only one in the Rigveda to Prthivi, Earth, though she is often celebrated with Dyaus, Heaven, conjointly, as a dual divinity. There is also a long and beautiful hymn addressed to Prthivi in the Atharvaveda.

The personification is but slight, as the attributes of the goddess are chiefly those of the physical earth. In a funeral hymn she is spoken of as "Kindly mother Earth," and when mentioned with Dyaus she frequently receives the epithet of "Mother." The name means "The broad one," being derived, as indicated in the Rigveda itself, from the root prath, "To extend."

PRITHVI: EARTH - HYMNS

Thou bearest truly, Prithvi,
The burden of the mountains' weight;
With might, O thouof many streams,
Thou quickenest, potent one, the soil,

With flowers of speech our songs of praise
Resound to thee, far-spreading one,
Who sendest forth the swelling cloud,
O bright one, like propelling speed;

Who, steadfast, boldest with thy might,
The forest-trees upon the ground,
When, from the lightning of thy cloud,
The rain-floods of the sky pour down.

AGNI

Agni and Soma are the two great ritual deities of the Rigveda. Judged by the number of hymns addressed to him, Agni is second in importance to Indra only, being invoked in at least 200. His anthropomorphism is only rudimentary, being connected chiefly with the sacrificial aspect of fire. He is butter-backed, flame-haired, has a tawny beard, sharp jaws, and golden teeth. His tongue, with which the gods eat the oblation, is often mentioned. With a burning head he faces in all directions.

Agni is compared with various animals: he resembles a bellowing bull, and sharpens his horns; when born he is often called a calf; when kindled he is like a horse that brings the gods, and is yoked to convey the sacrifice to them. He is also a divine bird; he is the eagle of the sky; as dwelling in the waters he is like a goose; he is winged and takes possession of the wood, as a bird perches on a tree.

AGNI - HYMNS

Agni I praise, the household priest,
God, minister of sacrifice,
Invoker, best bestowing wealth.

Agni is worthy to be praised,
By present as by seers of old:
May he to us conduct the gods.

Through Agni may we riches gain,
And day by day prosperity
Replete with fame and manly sons.

The worship and the sacrifice,
Guarded by thee on every side,
Go straight, O Agni, to the gods.

SOMA

As the Soma sacrifice forms the centre of the ritual of the Rigveda, this is one of the most prominent deities, coming next in importance to Agni, as indicated by the number of hymns addressed to him. His anthropomorphism is little developed, because the plant and its juice are constantly present to the mind and the vision of the poet.

Soma has sharp and terrible weapons, which he grasps in his hand; he wields a bow and a thousand-pointed shaft. He has a celestial car drawn by a team like Vayu's; he is also said to ride on the same car as Indra; and he is the best of charioteers. He is associated as a dual divinity in about half a dozen hymns with Indra, Agni, Ptisan and Rudra. He is sometimes attended by the Maruts, Indra's close allies. He comes to the sacrifice to receive the offerings, and seats himself on the sacred grass.

SOMA - HYMNS

I have partaken wisely of the sweet food
That stirs good thoughts, best banisher of trouble,
The food round which all deities and mortals.
Calling it honey-mead, collect together,

Thou shalt be Aditi when thou hast entered
Within, appeaser of celestial anger.
May'st thou, O drop, enjoying Indra's friendship,
Like willing mare the car, to wealth advance us.

We have drunk Soma and become immortal;
We have attained the light the gods discovered.
What can hostility now do against us?
And what, immortal god, the spite of mortals

YAJUR VEDA

INTRODUCTION

GENESIS OF THE VEDAS

Vedas are the Word of God, revealed in the beginning of creation for the moral, spiritual and physical guidance and uplift of humanity. They are replete with eternal truths and throw a flood of light on the various aspects of life to make a man perfect and ideal. God out of His infinite source of knowledge reveals in the beginning of creation a part of it adequate for the requirements of the soul, its spiritual satisfaction, fulfilment of its thirst for truth and making its journey of life successful.

God is infinite, the soul is finite. The finite soul cannot contain the infinite knowledge of God, God creates, sustains and dissolves the world. Whenever the world is created God reveals the Vedas. This processes going on since eternity and will go on for ever.

Maharshi Patanjali writes in the Mahabhashya, that there are 101 Shakhas (schools of thought) of the Yajurveda. All of these commentaries are not available at present except the Kanva, Madhyandini, Taitriya, Maitrayani, Kathak, and Kapishthal. On this point Maharshi Dayananda agrees with Patanjali.

There was a time when the learned Pundits memorised one or more Vedas, could recite or reproduce them from memory, but alas this system is no longer in vogue due to lack of public and state patronage.

The names of the Rishis attached to the Mantras are the names of those research scholars and seers, who expounded the meanings of the verses and commented upon them. They are not the authors or writers of those verses as the western scholars say. Devata is the subject matter of a verse, the topic discussed in it. All good men and beneficent forces of nature like air, fire, water, electricity, months, sun, moon, breaths, lightning, father, mother, teacher, preacher, and soul, which are beneficial to humanity are called devatas. They are not all living, personified beings as some erroneously believe them to be.

CHAPTER I

I

O, Lord, we resort to Thee for the supply of foodstuffs and vigour. May the Creator, the fountain of happiness and knowledge, inspire us for the performance of noblest deeds with our organs May the cows, which should never be killed, be healthy and strong. For the attainment of prosperity and wealth, may the cows be full of calves, free from consumption and other diseases. Maya thief and a sinner be never born amongst us. May the lord of land and cattle be in constant and full possession of these. May Ye protect the cattle, wealth and progeny of the virtuous soul.

II

Yajna acts as purifier, makes explicit, true and perfect knowledge, spread in space through the rays of the sun, purifies the air, is the mainstay of the universe, and also adds to our comfort through its exalted office. It behoves us all the learned and their followers not to give up the performance of yajnas.

III

The yajna of the Great Lord is the supporter of innumerable worlds and purifies us all. May the Self-Effulgent Lord, lead us aright on the path of virtue.

May He purify us through the store of true knowledge and all sciences contained in the Vedas, and elevating selfless deeds.

O ye men which branches of true knowledge do ye want to comprehend?

IV

Vedas are the true source of knowledge and their study enables us to enjoy the full span of life. They contain the detailed instructions concerning various duties. May we through His grace be firmly convinced of the utility of industrial achievements, and may He, the Omnipresent Lord protect our yajnas and the knowledge and means thereof.

V

O God, the Lord of Vows, I will observe the vow. May I have strength for that. Pray grant me success in the fulfilment of my vow. I take the vow of renouncing untruth and embracing truth.

VI

Who prompts you to do good deeds? It is He, the Great Lord who guides us on the path of virtue. Why does He do so ? For the performance of noble, virtuous deeds and the fulfilment of the vow of leading a truthful life. The Lord enjoins the workers and their organisers, the teacher and the taught to be constantly engaged in doing good deeds and achieving fine qualities and true knowledge.

VII

May we root out the evil tendencies of the wicked, the unsympathetic and uncharitable exploiters of humanity. May we take to task the disturbers of peace, and expose the wicked. May we thus get many an opportunity of attaining to prosperity and bliss.

VIII

O Lord, Thou art the dispeller of vices. May Thou punish - the wicked. May Thou deal with the vicious that put the sages to trouble. May Thou inspire the sinful with noble thought, whom we, too, exhort to do noble deeds. We worship Thee, the Giver of happiness and knowledge to the learned, purifier of them, the Promulgator of learning and joy in the universe, and worthy of adoration by the religious minded devotees and the wise.

IX

O Ye men, increase the store of goods acquired by honest and fair means to be used in the service of humanity. May your life, be constantly dedicated to this principle. May the spiritually minded people, also, not give up this humanitarian work. May your lives be constantly consecrated to the performance of five daily duties. The heat of the sun destroys dirt and odour, and draws substances consigned to fire, in their atomic form for the purification of air.

X

In this universe created by the All Effulgent God, I realize the power and influence of the sun and moon, feel the inhalation and exhalation of life-giving breath, appreciate the efforts made by the votaries of knowledge for mastering science of electricity. I follow the researches made by the learned in the applications of water and fire.

XI

I resort to agriculture and craft for removing poverty and ministering happiness to all. May I feel joy in my domestic life. May our houses be sufficiently commodious, airy, fully comfortable, and built in the middle of an open space. May our life be in conformity with Vedic teachings. O Lord we pray unto Thee to preserve and protect whatever gives us happiness.

XII

O learned persons, just as in this world created by God, inhaling and exhaling breaths are purified by the faultless and pure rays of the sun, just as charming and beautiful waters, which run to the ocean and go up in the atmosphere and nourish medicines are purified by these rays, so do ye perform Homa with pure substances. I always promote this yajna, and sanctify the worshipper with pure mind and strong body, the worshipper full of learning and noble qualities.

XIII

O performers of yajnas, as the sun receives the aforesaid waters and the air to dispel clouds, and absorbs them for the fast moving clouds, hence ye should always perform yajnas.

We all should perform agreeable yajnas, for the attainment of God, for noble acts, for the acquisition of fine virtues and for temporal and spiritual advancement. With the aid of yajnas purify all substances and human beings. Yajnas will remove all your physical and mental defects. I, the Revealer of the Veda, advance this purificatory act of yours.

XIV

May your house be comfortable. It should afford no shelter to the wicked and the uncharitable. May your house serve on as skin of the Earth. May all persons acquire such a house through the grace of God. Clouds receive moisture from forests, reside in the vast space, and receive water from air. May God impart you this knowledge of clouds and building houses. May the learned understand the building of houses, which serve as skin of the earth.

XV

O yajna, thou art the body of the fire. Thou art performed with the recitation of vedic verses, I perform thee for the acquisition of noble qualities. Thou art a great cloud, the fosterer of herbs, Cleanse this oblation, the assuager of mental pain, for the happiness of thelearned Cleanse it well. Those who read and teach the Vedas, become acquainted with the Vedic lore, inspiring us for the performance of yajnas.

XVI

The yajna keeps away the thieves, refines and sweetens the speech, is productive of foodstuffs and is the bestower of knowledge and vigour. Let the performance of such yajnas be inculcated. May we through the aid of heroic persons win battles again and again.

The yajna is instrumental in producing rain, may we know thee as rain producer. We should try to efface the dacoits and exploiters of impure minds who lead an impious life.

Just as the air with its strong hands of definite motion to and fro receives the oblations and just as the bright Sun full of luminous beams, with his faultless rays resolves into atoms the substances put into the fire, so do God and the scholars preach all sciences for the good of humanity.

XVII

O Lord, dauntless art Thou. Let us avoid in a yajna the use of fire that burns the corpses, and use the fire, that ripens the raw commodities, and endows us with nobler qualities. Through thy teachings remove our miseries and confer bliss on us.

XVIII

O Lord, Thou art the sustainer of the universe. Accept our adoration offered through Vedic verses and develop our inexhaustible mental knowledge. For the destruction of internal foes I realise Thee in my heart as the Supporter of the learned, the statesman and the Guide on the path of duty of different classes. Thou art the Supporter of the universe, we pray unto Thee to increase our knowledge. For the destruction of our internal foes, we realise Thee in our hearts as the Supporter of the learned, the statesman and the Guide on the path of duty of different classes. I imbibe in my heart Thee the All pervader, the Giver of happiness from all directions.

O Ye men, lead a life of penance by controlling your breath, and following the wise, the scientists and the learned.

XIX

The yajna is the giver of happiness, puts an end to the selfish and miserly habits and protects the mid-regions as skin protects the body. May the performer of the yajna realise its significance. The proper recitation of the vedic hymns is the yajna in itself. The yajna performed on special occasions also protects the truth as skin protects the body. The yajna is the sustainer of the illustrious sun, the embodiment of Vedic lore.

May we realise the yajna as the bringer of rain, and the giver of spiritual knowledge.

XX

The foodstuffs and water purified by the performance of yajna strengthen the body and sense organs. May we resort to yajna for sound health, for activities, for vitality, for long life full of happiness and prosperity. The glorious Creator and Emancipator of the universe, through His perfect Omnipresence, blesses us for the dissemination of true sublime knowledge.

XXI

O men, just as I the Lord, propagate the knowledge of this yajna in the world created by Me, and perform it through the bright sun, stable Earth, vitalizing air and various kinds of breaths in the human organism, so do ye. May you prepare, for your benefit, mixtures of different medicines with water and with juices and dilute the same again with distilled water. May you, thus, effect useful combinations of the beneficial medicines, with refined tinctures.

XXII

I fully harness the yajna for the attainment of happiness and material prosperity. This oblation is put into the fire, which expands, reaches in the middle region of the sun and moon and produces food-stuff.

The yajna confers fuller life and happiness. May this yajna be performed everywhere. May the performer of the yajna spread its knowledge. May the sacrificial Agni keep us free from diseases. May the indwelling Effulgent God, make our yajna perfect for the attainment of complete joys.

XXIII

Be fearless and do not waver as to the performance of yajna. Let the offspring of the performer of this yajna be excellent, faithful and free from weakness. We whole heartedly take recourse to yajnas for the realisation of the one Lord, for the purification of air and water and for getting the blessings of mother, father and preceptor.

XXIV

By the impulse of God the Giver of bliss, I perform the yajna free from Hinsa (violence), for the attainment of noble qualities and association of the learned, through the aid of life-giving-breath, vitalising air, and through the rejuvenating rays of the sun and moon. A yajna is the recipient of the rays of the sun that ripens a large variety of objects and is full of immense lustre, and innumerable rays. A yajna is the illuminating source of rain. With the aid of the yajna we should remove our miseries.

XXV

O God, the Creator of the solar and bright regions we implore Thee that through Thy grace, may we not destroy the medicinal herbs of the earth, on which the learned perform the yajnas. May the yajna reach the clouds. Let the sun pour rain on the earth through its rays.

O heroic persons bind by various fetters a wicked man in this world, who is opposed to us and is opposed to by us, and release him not.

XXVI

O' Omnipresent Lord, the Giver of happiness, may we subjugate the wicked folk on this earth where the sages perform yajnas. May we associate with the learned and, thus spread freely the system of education as propounded in the Vedic hymns. Just as My light of
knowledge is valued by all, so should yours. The ignorant moving in the dark who are opposed to the learned, and whom the learned disapprove for their antagonism to knowledge, should be brought round to the path of virtue by hundreds of means available and let the restriction on them be not removed till their enlightenment. May the wicked, be not
blessed with prosperity, and the pleasure of knowledge. O Ye dutiful may ye persistently follow the path of virtue.

CHAPTER II

I

Oh yajna, thou art being performed in a well dug place, them art i?refied by fire and attracted by the air. For the sake of Havan I consecrate the oblation agreeably rectified by thee. Thou art an alter for taking the oblations high up into the space; I erect thee and consecrate thee with ghee. Just jasjyater in the space contributes to the purification of the material objects, so do I carefully cleanse the oblations to be put into the fire ladles.

II

Yajna showers water on the Earth. Mortar is the chief receptacle of the yajna. I prepare the altar for the learned to sit on. May those scholars sing the praises of God, the Earth's Lord, the World's Lord, the Lord of Kings.

III

The sun is the sustainer of the world and the holder of the earth, spreads the yajna far and wide for the happiness of the universe. Adorable fire,

being adored in the yajna, thou art the guardian of the worshipper. O yajna thou art the inducer of rain through the power of sun for the happiness of the universe. Adorable fire, being adored in the yajna, thou art the guardian of the worshipper. Inhalation and exhalation, for the happiness of the universe, protect thee (yajna) with
firm strength every now and then. Adorable fire, being adored in the yajna, thou art the protector of the worshipper.

IV

May we, in a friendly spirit, manifest Thy glory Oh Omniscient, All-illumining God, the Giver of great happiness to all, the Embodiment of effulgence, and the Preacher of the yajnas.

V

Oh yajna, Thou art beautiful like the spring. The sun protects thee from time immemorial, for unfolding all objects. Thou art diffused through the power and potency (the two arms) of the sun. Just as Vasus, Rudras, and Adityas promote the yajna, the giver of happiness, pervaded in space, so do I for the acquisition of divine qualities, perform the yajna.

VI

Oh Yajna, thy name is sky, thou art full of butter, be confirmed in this decorated place with thy lovely glory. Oh Yajna thy name is space, thou art full of water, be confirmed in this decorated space with thy lovely glory. Oh Yajna thy name is Earth, thou art the giver of longevity, be confirmed in this decorated place with thy lovely glory. May necessary articles be placed in the holy yajna. O God, may Thou protect those articles, may Thou protect the Yajna, may Thou protect the worshipper, may Thou protect me the conductor of the Yajna.

VII

I kindle the fire, the giver of corn, full of intensity, the carrier of all oblations to the sky, and the bringer of victory in war. The fire properly used in the Yajna brings water through the forces of nature.

VIII

May I today for the acquisition of comforts collect through Yajna butter and other articles which contribute to happiness.

O God may I never violate it (Yajna). O Lord may I obtain Thy refuge, abounding in store of riches. This fire is the abode of yajna. Through it (yajna) sun and air gain strength. This yajna resides in space and fire.

IX

Oh God protect the sun and earth, which protect the yajna. Just as fire acquiring the yajna and acting as an envoy, protects the sun and earth, so protect us, Oh Lord the doer of the noble deeds for the learned. Just as the sun combining light with light through the oblations put into fire, protects the heaven and earth so God guard us with the light of spiritual knowledge. This is thus ordained in the Veda.

X

May God bestow on me spiritual power. May we obtain wealth full of various kinds of splendour, and earthly power. May our desires be fulfilled, may they attain to fruition, Men use this Earth and knowledge (whereby salvation is attained) for the pleasures of kingship. May these Earth and knowledge advise me. May God, as my last Refuge and resort instruct me. This is thus ordained in the Veda.

XI

I have prayed to the Effulgent, All sustaining God, May the Lord Father accept my prayer. Our digestive faculty digests by means of gastric juice the food put into the stomach. In this universe created by the All-Blissful God, I take that food through the qualities of attraction and retention, of inhalation and exhalation ; and the forces of purification and permeation of the invigorating air, throughout the body. Cooking my food in the burnt fire I eat it with my mouth.

XII

Oh Lord the Creator of the universe, the Vedas and the learned proclaim this fore-mentioned yajna of Thine for Brihaspati and Brahma. Through that great sacrifice protect my yajna, protect the performer of the yajna, protect Thou me.

XIII

May my active mind enjoy the yajna's provisions. May God expand and preserve this unabandonable acquisition of knowledge, which is a kind of yajna. May all the learned persons in the world rejoice. May Om be seated in our hearts.

XIV

Oh God, may Thou be glorified by our praises sung through Thy Vedas. May Thou promote our knowledge. Oh God, may we advance our soul. O God Thou controllest the activities of all. Thou art the embodiment of knowledge. Thou art Omniscient and the Bringer of victory in battles. May we prosper and sing Thy praises. I become pure and holy by following Thy commands.

XV

May I achieve victory like the victory of Fire and Moon. May I speed onward with the materials of war. May Fire and Moon, drive off him who hates us, drive off the man whom we detest. May I remove that sinful enemy by warlike, military skill and equipment. May I achieve victory like the victory of Air and Lightning. May I achieve happiness through the impulse of knowledge, used for the acquisition of supremacy. May air and lightning properly employed, drive off him who hates us, drive of the man whom we dislike. I purify this ignorant person by the light of knowledge.

XVI

We perform the yajna for Vasus, Rudras and Adityas. The light of the sun and earth bring thee (yajna) to light. The Pran (external air) and Udan (internal air) protect thee through rain. Just as birds go to their nests, so let us daily go to the yajna reciting Gayatri Mantras.

XVII

Oh Omnipresent God, extolled by the praises of the learned, Thou attainest to greatness through those lovely panegyrics. I realise that greatness of Thine in my heart. May I never disobey Thee. May I, Oh God, never abuse the pleasant and invigorating food, I have secured in Thy creation.

XVIII

May ye thriving, justice loving, wise, learned persons, preachers of the knowledge of the Vedas, become supreme through knowledge. Let all seekers after truth, devotees of learning and action, attain to happiness. Preach My noble word, that brings all kinds of joys.

XIX

Oh fire and air, ye are the bringers of rain. Ye protect the yajna, and conduce to our comfort, bring comfort to me. God and humility are near me for my good, as they are for thine. Just as I derive happiness by the performance of yajna, so should you.

XX

Oh Immortal, Omnipresent God, protect me from intense pain, protect me from the bondages of sin and ignorance, protect me from the company of evil-minded persons, protect me from food injurious to health. Make Thou our food free from poison. Let me live in a comfortable house; praying to Thee and doing noble needs. This is our prayer to the Lord of the Universe, may we get pure knowledge through the vedas, the givers of glory and prosperity.

XXI

Oh God, Thou knowest the animate and the inanimate creation. Thou knowest everything in the universe. Just as Thou art the expounder of knowledge for the learned, so dost Thou expound knowledge unto me. Ye learned people, who know how to sing praises unto God, knowing the veda that shows the right path, should master knowledge.

Oh God, the Master of learning, rightfully fix this yajnalike world in the air.

XXII

May the mighty space unite with oblation and butter. May it unite with the twelve months of the year, and eight lifegiving agencies and vital breaths, May the sun be harnessed with all its rays. May pure water rain whenever duly consecrated oblations are offered.

XXIII

Does anybody abandon the sacrifice? He who abandons it, is abandoned by God. For what purpose does the worshipper put the oblations into the fire? He does it for the happiness of all. He does it for gaining strength, health and vigour. The inferior articles not used in the sacrifice are the allotted portion of the fiends.

XXIV

May we be endowed with the study of the Vedas, knowledge, stout bodies, peaceful and devoted minds. May God, the Giver of happiness grant us riches, and banish each blemish from our body.

XXV

The Yajna performed by us in Jagati metre goes up to the sky. From there it is sent back and pleases the world. By means of this Yajna, may we ward off the man who hates us, and him whom we detest.
The yajna performed by us in Trishtup metre goes up in the air. From there it is released and affords happiness to the world by the purification of air and water. By means of this yajna, we keep away the man who hates us, and him whom we dislike. The yajna performed by us in Gayatri metre spreads on the Earth, and being released from there goes up to heaven, and purifies the objects of the Earth. By

means of this yajna we remove the man who hates us, and him whom we despise. By the use of food purified through yajna, may we get happiness, for the accomplishment of the yajna, and be combined with lustre.

XXVI

Oh God Thou art Self-Existent, Most Excellent, and Self-Effulgent, Giver art thou of knowledge. Give me knowledge. I follow the command of God.

XXVII

Oh Lord of the universe, Oh God, may I become a good householder through Thee, the protector of the universe. Oh Lord may Thou protect my house, being adored by me the guardian of my house. May our domestic duties be performed free from idleness. May I live for a hundred years day and night in the presence of God.

XXVIII

Oh God, the Lord of vows, pray grant me success in the performance of the vows, which I have undertaken, and which I find myself confident. I reap as I sow.

XXIX

Speak reverentially to the learned, the repository of knowledge. Speak sweetly and gently to your father, mother, teacher and the Brahmchari.
Extemnate all fiends and evil-minded persons in the world.

XXX

Oh God remove from this world the demoniacal beings who walk on the earth, dissembling their real intentions, who are immersed in the attainment of their selfish aims, and are filled with evil ambitions.

XXXI

In this world, let the wise and the learned enjoy, let them be strong, healthy and pleased, according to their capacity. Let them be happy, hale and hearty according to their resources.

XXXII

Obeisance unto Yee, O Fathers, for the acquisition of happiness and knowledge. Obeisance unto Yee, O Fathers for the removal of misery and enemies. Obeisance unto Yee, O Fathers for longevity, Obeisance unto Yee, O Fathers, for sovereignty, and display of justice. Obeisance unto Yee, O Fathers, for the cessation of manifold calamities.

XXXIII

Accept thou teacher, in the womb of thy discipleship, the youth, with a garland of flowers in hand, eager for knowledge, so that he may attain to full manhood.

XXXIV

Oh sons, please my parents and teachers by offering them various juices, sweet waters, disease dissipating articles, milk, clarified butter, well-cooked food, and juicy fruits. Enjoy your own wealth, and covet not the wealth of others.

CHAPTER III

I

Oh learned persons, kindle the fire with the wood sticks, with butter, set ablaze the fire, which is worthy of respect like a Sanyasi. Put oblations in this fire of the yajna.

II

Put the oblations of ghee that removes physical infirmities, into this well ablaze, disease-killing fire present in all objects.

III

We fan with sticks of wood and ghee the fire, that is powerful 8in splitting all things, and burns intensely.

IV

O beautiful fire, wood sticks soaked with ghee go unto thee along with oblations. May thou accept my fuel put into thee.

V

I lay upon the back of the Earth upon which the learned perform yajna, which is like Heaven in plenty, and like Earth in grandeur, for gain of eatable food, this food-eating fire, that pervades the Earth, Ether, and Sky.

VI

This Earth revolves in the. space, jt revolves with its mother water in its orbit.

VII

The lustre of this fire, goes up and comes down in the space like exhalation and inhalation in the body. This great fire displays the Sun.

VIII

God's word rules supreme throughout the world. The Vedas arc recited for acquiring the knowledge of God. We should resolutely recite and understand the Vedas everyday with their illuminating sayings.

IX

Just as God gives the light of truthful speech to all human beings, so does physical fire give light that illumines all substances. Just as God inculcates knowledge in the souls of all, that man should speak, as he feels in his heart, so does the Sun bring to light all physical objects. Just as God reveals for humanity all the four Vedas, the storehouse of knowledge, so does exist in the space, and become

the source of rain and knowledge.
Just as God, through the Vedas displays all sciences, fire, and lightning, so does the Sun develop our physical and spiritual forces. Sun illumines all objects. God is self-Resplendent. This is the manifestation of His Glory.

X

This enjoyable fire, in accompaniment with the recital of Vedic texts, mixed with God's creation and dark night, with flashes of lightning pervades all objects.
This sun, mixed with God's creation and brilliant dawn, receives the oblations put into the fire, and carries them to places far and wide.

XI

Performing sacrifice, may we pronounce vedic texts, in praise of God, who hears us from far and near.

XII

Men should worship God alone, who is the Great and Supreme Lord, who sustains the luminous Sun, and the non-luminous Earth, who knows the formation of the vitality of waters.

XIII

Oh Electricity and Fire, I invoke Ye both for knowing your attributes, for enjoying the pleasures of riches. Ye both are the givers of desired sovereignty. Ye twain I invoke for consuming excellent food.

XIV

Oh God, in Thy creation, sacrificial fire, whose cause of birth is air, burns in different seasons, and develops in all directions. Knowing this, cause our riches increase.

XV

In this world the instructors and the learned kindle in serviceable yajnas, for mankind, the ubiquitous fire of extra-ordinary qualities.
That fire is recognised by the regulators of sacrifice as worthy of adoration, as the first means of the performance of a yajna, as the receiver of sacrifice aad giver of happiness and scientific knowledge.

XVI

The learned, knowing the eternity, lustre, thousandfold service, and usefulness of fire, get pure water from it.

XVII

Thou. God, art our bodies 1 protector. Protect Thou my body.
Giver of longevity art Thou, O God, Give me longevity.
Giver of splendour art Thou, O God, Give me splendour.

Remove, O God, all the defects of my body and soul.

XVIII

Oh God, the Lord of manifold riches, may we, being free from pride, enjoying long life, and practising forbearance, live for a hundred years, praising Thee the Effulgent, the Eternal, the Forbearing, the Unconquerable, and the Killer of foes.
Through Thy kindness, being free from woes, may we attain to happiness.

XIX

Oh God, Thou art full of splendour like the Sun, sung by the sages with vedic verses, and O Thou full of power for protection May I attain to long life, to splendour, to offspring, and abundant riches.

XX

May I enjoy the life-bestowing food through the plants and medicines that contribute to health and vigour. May I utilise the science of air and water for the accomplishment of my deeds. May I get the essence of food from milk, honey and fruits. May I enjoy the 7abundance of good articles through objects full of manifold qualities.

XXI

Oh Vedic speech, may thou remain in this altar in this yajnd, in this spot and in this house. Remain here, and go not far from hence.

XXII

Oh universal vedic text, thou art full of vigour and valour, may we attain unto thee, the master of the yajna. O God, may we be in communion with Thee, everyday, morning and evening, bowing unto Thee through our intellect.

XXIII

May we worship God, Who is the Guardian of sacrifices, Radiant, the Revealer of the vedas, and attained to complete redemption.

XXIV

Oh God, Thou givest unto us knowledge, as a father to his son. Unite us perpetually with pleasure.

XXV

Oh God, Thou art the Bestower on us of ears to hear goodness, the Shelter of mankind, the Embodiment of the lustre of knowledge, and real Omnipresence. Thou pervadest our soul. Thou art our Protector, Our Benefactor, and possessest excellent nature, attributes and deeds. Give us wealth most splendidly renowned.

XXVI

O most pure, O radiant God, verily do we pray to Thee for the happiness of our friends. Give us knowledge, listen to our praises and prayers, and keep us far from every evil.

XXVII

O God, may I get land for ruling over it, may I be endowed with statesmanship. May noble desires reside in me. May I be the centre of the fulfilment of all ambitions.

XXVIII

O God, the Guardian of the primordial vedas, make me, like the son of a learned person, endowed with different capacities for the acquisition of knowledge, an imparter of instruction, and a fulfiller of the aim of education.

XXIX

God is rich and the dispeller of ignorance. He knows the true nature of all things, and grants us physical and spiritual strength. He is prompt. May he goad us to noble deeds.

XXX

O God, may not our knowledge of the Vedas ever perish. May thou preserve us from the violence of the uncharitable person.

XXXI

God, may we get the great, wise and unassailable protection of the three forces of nature, the water, the sun and the air.

XXXII

Those who worship God are not molested by evil-minded foes neither at home, nor upon pathways and battlefields. I become capable of acquiring God and the sages.

XXXIII

They, the sons of indestructible matter, bestow eternal light upon man for his life and death.

XXXIV

O God, Thou art the giver of happiness. If Thou dost not bestow knowledge promptly on a charitable person, he again, O Liberal Lord, does not attain to Thy bounty.

XXXV

O Creator of the Universe I O All holy and worthy of adoration! May we meditate on Thy adorable self. May Thou guide our understanding.

XXXVI

Oh God, may Thine immortal knowledge, wherewith Thou guardest the learned in all directions, come close from all sides.

XXXVII

O God, friendly to the wise, do Thou protect my offspring. O worthy of praise do Thou protect my cattle. O God, above all suspicion, protect my food. O God, through Thy grace, in unison with the three life-winds, Pran, Apan and Vyan, may I be rich in offspring, well-manned with men, a hero with the heroes, and strong with wise and invigorating deeds.

XXXVIII

O, Ocean of Light, the Omniscient, the best knower of all the worlds, and enjoyments may we well approach Thee. May Thou spread for us splendour and strength in all directions.

XXXIX

Lord of our houses, O God, Thou art the best finder of riches for our children, Thou art the protector of our hearths, and the companion of the householders. Bestow splendour and strength on us.

XL

This fire assists us in the accomplishment of our deeds. It is rich, and furtherer of plenty. O God, the Giver of our comforts, bestow splendour and strength upon us.

XLI

Fear not, nor tremble Ye, O householders. We, bearing strength, come to Ye. May I bearing strength, intelligent and happy, rejoicing in my mind, enjoy all pleasures and approach the householders.

XLII

We praise the householders, whom the guest staying far from home remembers and whom he loves much. The loving householders welcome us, the religious guests.

XLIII

May we in this world get cows, goats, sheep and abundant food in our houses. I come to you for safety and quietude, May I acquire mundane and celestial joy and felicity.

XLIV

We invocate the guests, who are delightful, free from ignorance, removers of sins, eaters of the food well cooked, and full of knowledge.

XLV

May we forsake each sinful act that we have committed in village or solitude, in an assembly or corporeal sense. Let every man so resolve.

XLVI

O God, protect us in battles, in this world, with the help of heroes and destroy us not.

XLVII

They, who with delightful vedic voice, working in cooperation, perform their desired deeds, go to their comfortable house, after the completion of their task for the acquisition of noble virtues.

XLVIII

O purified through knowledge and righteousness, O patient teacher of grammar, just as I a seeker after knowledge, and a firm gleaner of wisdom, wash out the sin that I have committed through my senses and the mortal body, so do thou O God, preserve me from tortuous sin.

XLIX

The oblation full of cooked articles put into the fire, goes up to the sky. and returns therefrom full of rain.

O God, Let us twain, like traders, barter our food and strength.

L

Give me this article and I will give you that in return. Keep this as my deposit, I keep this as your deposit. Give me the cash price for it. I give you the price demanded. Let people thus transact business truthfully.

LI

Thou chairman, just as comrades, luminous in themselves, pleasing others, advanced in knowledge, with their sharpest intellect, do verily praise God, and being regaled with nutritious diet, overcome miseries, so do thou yoke thy vigour and prowess with them.

LII

We revere Thee, O God of Bounty, Who art fair to see. Being praised by us, O best companion, Thou fulfillest all our desires. O Lord, yoke Thy vigour and prowess for us.

LIII

May we get in future births again and again the mind, for doing virtuous deeds, for acquiring strength, for longevity, and contemplation of God'for long.

LIV

O venerable elders, may this man endowed with godly qualities, give us in this and the next life, intellect whereby we may enjoy a long life and perform noble deeds.

LV

O God, acting upon Thy Law, possessing mental self-consciousness in healthy bodies, blest with progeny, let us enjoy happiness.

LVI

O learned person, the chastiser of the sinful and the unrighteous, all these eatable things are for thee. Accept them with thy knowledge and vedic lore. O learned man, follow the Veda and the law of Dharma. O learned person, accept the food worth eating which uproots all diseases.

LVII

May we ward off all calamities by worshipping God, Who is unchangeable in the past, presenr and future, chastises the sinners, and is highly benevolent. Just as God makes us better housed, more prosperous, and determined so may we adore Him.

LVIII

O God, Thou art the healer of the physical, mental and spiritual maladies. Heal, Thou the sufferings of cow, horse and all mankind. Grant happiness to ram and ewe.

LVIX

O hero, the chastiser of enemies, and expert in the art of war, with bow extended, with self-protecting trident, with full armour, with grace and power, meet thy foes on the other side of the mountain. With thy this power of prote tion, come to us, without causing us any harm.

LX

May we be endowed with triple life, as a truth-seer sage, or the custodian of knowledge through the grace of God, is endowed with, or as the learned persons enjoy triple life.

CHAPTER IV

I

May we, on this earth, where reside happily all the learned persons, be able to revere the sages.
May we acting on the teachings of the Rig, Sam and Yajur Vedas, end all our miseries. May we rejoice in food and growth of riches. These pure, disease-killing waters be gracious to me. May the herbs protect me Thou armed king, harm not the worshipper.

II

May waters, like mother, purify our bodies. May the waters purified by clarified butter, purify us through rain. Pure waters remove all our physical imperfections.
May I advance in life, being bright and pure through waters. Through celibacy and absteniousness may I possess a body, healthy, comfortable, excellent, beautiful and strong.

III

O Sun, thou bringest rain on different parts of the earth. Giver of splendour art thou bestow on me the gift of splendour. The disperser of cloud art thou with thy brilliance. The giver of eye art thou. Give we the gift of vision.

IV

Purify me, the Lord of Purity. Purify me, the Lord of knowledge, Purify me, the Lord of the Vedas.
O Lord, Creator of the universe, purify me, through sun-beams and thy immortal purifying knowledge.
O Master of the purified souls, may I full of lofty sentiments accomplish the desire actuated by which, through your grace, I purify myself.

V

O sages, we admire your praiseworthy qualities, during the performance of this happy sacrifice. O sages, we beg of you the fulfilment of our desires pertaining to the sacrifice.

VI

O men, just as I actively and wisely commence performing the sacrifice, with vedic texts, with cultured tongue, with wisdom teaching voice, with a tongue full of sweetness and truth, in an orderly and well-directed way, with the help of the extended firmament, Earth, sky and air, so do Ye.

VII

We perform the yajna for resolution for good religious acts, for kindling fire, for the propagation of the Vedas, for the development of wisdom, for the enhancement of knowledge, for utilizing lightning, for philanthropy, for following the laws of Dharma, for austerity, for digestive faculty, for learning and teaching, for eloquent and weighty speech, for worshipping rightly God, for purifying gastric juice, and for practising Truth. Ye, meritorious, all-beneficial divine waters, Ye Heaven and Earth and spacious air between them, we serve with Oblation.

VIII

May every mortal man seek the friendship of the Guiding God.

May we all have recourse to the use of arms for the acquisition of due wealth. May every man acquire riches and become strong through wise deeds.

IX

After the study of the Rig and Yajur Vedas, I commence using their scientific aspects, i.e., theoretical and practical.

In this yajna, in which vedic texts are recited. O yajna, thou art happiness, give me happiness; here are these oblations of corn for thee; forbear to harm me.

X

O learned person, may mechanical science, perfected by the application of fire, the giver of light, bestow strength on me. It is the guardian of manifold objects, giver of happiness to the learned, the mechanic, and the source of prosperity, make the crops produce abundant grain through its aid. O learned person, depend on thyself for advancement. Protect me from the misery of sin. Accomplish this yajna with the recitation of vedic texts.

XI

Take a vow. God is Agni. Yajna is Agni. God, the Guardian of our soul, is fit for worship. For the attainment of an ideal, I long for divine, pleasant, radiant intelligence that unites me with God. May that intelligence, that makes me happily cross the ocean of this mundane existence, be within my control.

May the philosophic, meditative and energetic sages urge us on to noble deeds, may they be our protectors. We invoke them from the inmost recesses of our heart.

XII

O men, the waters that we have ,lrunk, staying within our belly, give us peace, riches, freedom from consumption, disease, and pangs of hunger and thirst. They are the strengthened of our true knowledge, full of divine qualities, and undying flavours. May they be pleasant to your taste.

XIII

O learned man, just as this sacrificial body of thine, protects the vital breaths and the people, and thou forsakest it not, so do I not forsake it without enjoying the full span of life. Just as disease curing and pure waters flow on the earth, so shouldst thou live in the world wisely; and so do I.

XIV

The fire, which keeps us active in our wakeful state, makes us take joy in most refreshing sleep. It protects us free from idleness and casts away the idlers. We should use this fire properly which deals with us again and again.

XV

I get back after rebirth mind, life, bre.ith, soul, eyes and ears.
May God the Leader of all, Non-violent, Omniscient, Guardian of our souls, save us from misfortune and sin.

XVI

O God, Thou art the Guardian of sacred vows among mankind. Thou art meet for praise at holy rites. O Giver of Splendour, Come unto us, grant us wealth, give us more. God, the Creator, the Giver of wealth, gives us riches.

XVII

O learned person, this body thou hast got and reared is for the meditation of God and sacrifice. Through this body, being vigorous, gain splendour and lustre. Be active through knowledge.

XVIII

O resplendent God, in this world created by Thee, may I obtain mastery over the vast power of speech. O Speech, thou art pure, pleasant and dear to the sages.

XIX

O Speech, thou art thought, mind, intelligence, giver of knowledge and victory ; thou art power, worthy of worship, immortal, and double-headed. May thou give us comfort in the past and future. May breath, the strength giving friend of time advance thee in knowledge, and guard thy pathways for God, whose eye is over all.

XX

O man, may thy mother, thy father, thy own brother, and thy friend of the same society grant thee leave to tread on the path ordained by God. O speech, for the acquisition of splendour, may thou unite with God, the Prompter of all. May the Celibate student choose thee. May thou, O man, happily acquire again and again this speech, the friend of the learned.

XXI

O speech, thou art all-pervading, eternal, lustrous, sublime and pleasant. The learned person uses thee for happiness. The sage, the chastiser of the wicked longs for thee along with other educated persons.

XXII

O speech, I use thee in the heights of sky and the sacrificial places on the Earth. Thou art the preserver of vedic verses. May thou be enriched with high knowledge. May thou rest in us. May thou be united to us. Thou art rich. May I be full of riches. Let us not be deprived of abundant riches. May splendour reside in thee full of understanding.

XXIII

O speech, I praise thee with divine, ignorance removing and penetrating intelligence. End not my life. I will not through ignorance spoil thee. O vedic text, in thy protection, may I be blessed with heroism.

XXIV

O learned person "This is thy share of the sacrifice allied with Gayatri verses" so may he say unto me a student of science.This is thy share of the sacrifice allied with Trishtup verses/ so may he say unto me, the seeker of the essence of things. This is thy share of the sacrifice allied with verses in Jagati metre/ so may he say unto me a student of science. 'May thou attain to sovereignty detailed in vedic-verses in all other metres/ May he thus preach the art of kingship unto me, full of affluence, O learned persons, just as ye are our purifying preachers, so am I your worthy disciple, endowed with virtues and wealth. May ye develop me and this sacrifice (yajna) as well.

XXV

I adore God, the Creator of the Earth and Sky, the Source of all Knowledge, the Embodiment of Splendour, the Sustainer of all the beautiful planets, the Centre of love, the object of praise by the Vedas, and their Revealer. His lofty effulgent Self is divulged in the created world. He has fixed the bright sun and the moon in their conduct. He is the wisest Actor. His mercy grants us happiness. O God I worship Thee as Bestower of happiness on mankind. May all mortals enjoy life, through Thee. May Thou grant life to all human beings.

XXVI

In the yajna, we should please the learned performer by offering him cash and kind. May the praiseworthy brilliance of the sun make me strong through its thousandfold abundance. O wise person, may we also obtain the riches, which thou hast secured through thy rule over the earth. Just as I accomplish the sacrifice through noble, pure sentiments, earn gold with gold, attain to salvation through immortal knowledge, so may thou.

XXVII

O king, famous for eloquence, brilliance, enmity to fraud, antagonism to the thoughtless, pleasing manners, dexterity, defeating the designs of the ill-minded, friendship, and the art of befriending others, with longing for delight, come into us.
May thou, with a beautiful and healthy body, and endowed with all cherished objects, enjoy enviable happiness. These intelligent and faith-full subjects and servants, who all round protect you, should be protected by you to ward off your enemy from doing injury unto you.

XXVIII

Oh God, dissuade me from sin, and establish me firmly in righteousness. May I enjoy the pleasures of final beatitude by leading a long and virtuous life.

XXIX

May we tread the path free from sin, and full of delight, by which a wise man overcomes all carnal pleasures, and gathers wealth.

XXX

O God, Thou art the protector of the Earth, O Mighty Lord, Thou fixed the Earth in its Orbit. Thou Controllest the Sun. Thou hast created the beautiful sky. O Lord of all, thou fixest in space all the worlds. All these are the works of Him alone, so do we know.

XXXI

We should worship God, who hast created the sky over the forests, put speed in horses, milk in cows, intellect in hearts, gastric juice in men, sun in heaven, and medicinal plants like Soma in the mountains.

XXXII

O God, where resplendent through Thy qualities of knowledge, Thou art known by the learned, and where Thou Greatest lustrous eyes, the instruments for seeing the sun and fire, there we worship Thee.

XXXIII

Let man and woman, who study the vedas kill not their heroes, are limited in resources, be ever joyous, who live together and are fit to bear the burden of domestic life, be united together in married life. May such couples visit the houses of religious persons and give them happiness.

SAMA VEDA

PART I
BOOK I
CHAPTER I

Om. Glory to the Samaveda! To Lord Ganesa glory!
Om.

DECADE I - AGNI

1.

Come, Agni, praised with song, to feast and
sacrificial offering: sit
As Hotar on the holy grass!

2.

O Agni, thou hast been ordained
Hotar of every sacrifice,
By Gods, among the race of men.

3.

Agni we choose as envoy, skilled performer of
this holy rite,
Hotar, possessor of all wealth.

4.

Served with oblation, kindled, bright, through love
of song may Agni, bent
On riches, smite the Vritras dead!

5.

I laud your most beloved guest like a dear friend,
O Agni, him
Who, like a chariot, wins us wealth.

6.

Do thou, O Agni, with great might guard us
from all malignity,
Yea, from the hate of mortal man!

7.

O Agni, come; far other songs of praise
will I sing forth to thee.
Wax mighty with these Soma-drops!

8.

May Vatsa draw thy mind away even from thy
loftiest dwelling place!
Agni, I yearn for thee with song.

9.

Agni, Atharvan brought thee forth by rubbing from
the sky, the head
Of all who offer sacrifice.

10.

O Agni, bring us radiant light to be our mighty
succour, for
Thou art our visible deity!

DECADE II - AGNI

1.

O Agni, God, the people sing reverent
praise to thee for strength:
With terrors trouble thou the foe

2.

I seek with song your messenger,
oblation-bearer, lord of wealth,
Immortal, best at sacrifice.

3.

Still turning to their aim in thee
the sacrificer's sister hymns
Have come to thee before the wind.

4.

To thee, illuminer of night,
O Agni, day by day with prayer,
Bringing thee reverence, we come.

5.

Help, thou who knowest lauds, this work,
a lovely hymn in Rudra's praise,
Adorable in every house!

6.

To this fair sacrifice to drink the milky draught art
thou called forth:
O Agni, with the Maruts come!

7.

With homage will I reverence thee, Agni,
like a long-tailed steed,
Imperial lord of holy rites.

8

As Aurva and as Bhrigu called,
as Apnavana called, I call
The radiant Agni robed with sea.

9.

When he enkindles Agni, man should with his heart
attend the song:
I kindle Agni till he glows.

10.

Then, verily, they see the light
refulgent of primeval seed,
Kindled on yonder side of heaven.

DECADE III - AGNI

1.

Hither, for powerful kinship, I call Agni,
him who prospers you,
Most frequent at our solemn rites.

2.

May Agni with his pointed blaze cast down each
fierce devouring fiend:
May Agni win us wealth by war!

3.

Agni, be gracious; thou art great: thou hast
approached the pious man,
Hast come to sit on sacred grass.

4.

Agni, preserve us, from distress consume our
enemies, O God,
Eternal, with thy hottest flames

5.

Harness, O Agni, O thou God, thy steeds which are most excellent!
The fleet ones bring thee rapidly.

6.

Lord of the tribes, whom all must seek, we worshipped Agni set thee down,
Refulgent, rich in valiant men.

7.

Agni is head and height of heaven, the master of the earth is he
He quickeneth the waters' seed.

8.

O Agni, graciously announce this our good fortune of the Gods,
And this our newest hymn of praise!

9.

By song, O Agni, Angiras! Gopavana hath brought thee forth
Hear thou my call, refulgent one!

10.

Agni, the Sage, the Lord of Strength, hath moved around the sacred gifts,
Giving the offerer precious things.

11.

His heralds bear him up aloft, the God who knoweth all that lives,
The Sun, that all may look on him.

12.

Praise Agni in the sacrifice, the Sage whose holy laws are true
The God who driveth grief away.

13.

Kind be the Goddesses to lend us help, and kind that we may drink:
May their streams bring us health and wealth

14.

Lord of the brave, whose songs dost thou in thine abundance now inspire,
Thou whose hymns help to win the kine?

DECADE IV - AGNI

1.

Sing to your Agni with each song,
at every sacrifice for strength.
Come, let us praise the wise and, everlasting God
even as a well-beloved friend.

2.

Agni, protect thou us by one, protect us by the
second song,
Protect us by three hymns, O Lord of power and
might, bright God, by four hymns guard us well!

3.

O Agni, with thy lofty beams, with thy pure
brilliancy, O God,
Kindled, most youthful one! by Bharadvaja's hand,
shine on us richly, holy Lord!

4.

O Agni who art worshipped well, dear let our
princes be to thee,
Our wealthy patrons who are governors of men,
who part, as gifts, the stall of kine!

5.

Agni, praise-singer! Lord of men, God!
Burning up the Rakshasas,
Mighty art thou, the ever-present, household-lord!
home-friend and guardian from the sky.

6.

Immortal Jatavedas, thou bright-hued refulgent
gift of Dawn,
Agni, this day to him who pays oblations bring the
Gods who waken with the morn!

7.

Wonderful, with thy favouring help, send us thy
bounties, gracious Lord.
Thou art the charioteer, Agni, of earthly wealth:
find rest and safety for our seed!

8.

Famed art thou, Agni, far and wide, preserver,
righteous, and a Sage.
The holy singers, O enkindled radiant one,
ordainers, call on thee to come.

9.

O holy Agni, give us wealth famed among
men and strengthening life!
Bestow on us, O helper, that which many crave,
more glorious still through righteousness!

10.

To him, who dealeth out all wealth, the sweet-toned
Hotar-priest of men,
To him like the first vessels filled with savoury
juice, to Agni let the lauds go forth.

DECADE V - AGNI

1.

With this mine homage I invoke Agni for you,
the Son of Strength,
Dear, wisest envoy, skilled in noble sacrifice,
immortal messenger of all.

2.

Thou liest in the logs that are thy mothers:
mortals kindle thee.
Alert thou bearest off the sacrifleer's gift, and then
thou shinest to the Gods.

3.

He hath appeared, best prosperer,
in whom men lay their holy acts:
So may our songs of praise come nigh to Agni who
was born to give the Arya strength!

4.

Chief Priest is Agni at the laud,
as stones and grass at sacrifice.
Gods! Maruts! Brahmanaspati! I crave with song
the help that is most excellent.

5.

Pray Agni of the piercing flame,
with sacred songs, to be our help;
For wealth, famed Agni, Purumilha and ye men!
He is Suditi's sure defence.

6.

Hear, Agni who hast ears to hear,
with all thy train of escort Gods!
With those who come at dawn let Mitra, Aryaman
sit on the grass at sacrifice.

7.

Agni of Divodasa, God, comes forth like
Indra in his might.
Rapidly hath he moved along his mother earth: he
stands in high heaven's dwelling-place.

8.

Whether thou come from earth or from the lofty
lucid realm of heaven,

Wax stronger in thy body through my song of
praise: fill full all creatures, O most wise!

9.

If, loving well the forests, thou wentest to thy
maternal floods,
Not to be scorned, Agni, is that return of thine
when, from afar, thou now art here.

10.

O Agni, Manu stablished thee a light
for all the race of men:
With Kanva hast thou blazed, Law-born and waxen
strong, thou whom the people reverence.

CHAPTER II
DECADE I - AGNI

1.

The God who giveth wealth accept your full libation
poured to, him!
Pour ye it out, then fill the vessel full again,
for so the God regardeth you.

2.

Let Brahmanaspati come forth, let
Sunrita the Goddess come,
And Gods bring to our rite which yields a fivefold
gift the hero, lover of mankind!

3.

Stand up erect to lend us aid, stand up like
Savitar the God,
Erect as strength-bestower when we call on thee
with priests who balm our offerings!

4.

The man who bringeth gifts to thee, bright God who
fain wouldst lead to wealth,
Winneth himself a brave son, Agni! skilled in lauds,
one prospering in a thousand ways.

5.

With hymns and holy eulogies we supplicate
your Agni, Lord
Of many families who duly serve the Gods, yea,
him whom others too inflame.

6.

This Agni is the Lord
of great prosperity and hero, strength,
Of wealth with noble offspring and with store of
kine, the Lord of battles with the foe.

7.

Thou, Agni, art the homestead's Lord, our
Hotar-priest at sacrifice.
Lord of all boons, thou art the Potar, passing wise.
Pay worship, and enjoy the good!

8.

We as thy friends have chosen thee,
mortals a God, to be our help.
The Waters' Child, the blessed, the most mighty
one, swift conqueror, and without a peer.

DECADE II - AGNI

1.

Present oblations, make him splendid: set ye as
Hotar in his place the Home's Lord, worshipped
With gifts and homage where they pour libations!
Honour him meet for reverence in our houses.

2.

Verily wondrous is the tender youngling's growth
who never draweth nigh to drink his mother's milk.
As soon as she who hath no udder bore him, he,
faring on his. great errand, suddenly grew strong.

3.

Here is one light for thee, another yonder: enter the
third and, be therewith united.
Beautiful be thy union with the body, beloved in the
Gods' sublimest birthplace!

4.

For Jatavedas, worthy of our praise, will we frame
with our mind this eulogy as 'twere a car;
For good, in his assembly, is this care of ours. Let
us not, in thy friendship, Agni, suffer harm!

5.

Agni Vaisvanara, born in course of Order, the
messenger of earth, the head of heaven,
The Sage, the sovran, guest of men, our vessel fit
for their mouth, the Gods have generated.

6.

Even as the waters from the mountain ridges, so
sprang the; Gods, through lauds, from thee, O Agni.
To thee speed hymns and eulogies, as horses haste,
bearing him who loves the song, to battle.

7.

Win to protect you, Rudra, lord of worship, priest of
both worlds, effectual sacrificer,
Agni, invested with his golden colours, before the
thunder strike and lay you senseless!

8.

The King whose face is decked with oil is kindled
with homage offered by his faithful servant.
The men, the priests adore him with oblations. Agni
hath shone forth at the flush of morning.

9.

Agni advanceth with his lofty banner: through earth and heaven the Bull hath loudly bellowed
He hath come nigh from the sky's farthest limit: the Steer hath waxen in the waters' bosom.

10.

From the two fire-sticks have the men engendered with thoughts, urged by the hand, the glorious Agni,
Far-seen, with pointed flame,
Lord of the Homestead.

DECADE III - AGNI

1.

Agni is wakened by the people's fuel to meet the
Dawn who cometh like a milch-cow.
Like young trees shooting up on high
their branches, his flames.

2.

Set forth the gleaming one, the song-inspirer, not
foolish with. the foolish, fort-destroyer,
Who leadeth with his hymns to thought of conquest,
gold-bearded, richly splendid with his armour

3.

Thou art like heaven: one form is bright, one holy,
like Day and Night dissimilar in colour.
All magic powers thou aidest, self-dependent!
Auspicious bethy bounty here, O Pushan!

4.

As holy food, Agni, to thine invoker give wealth in cattle, lasting, rich in marvels!
To us be born a son and spreading offspring. Agni, be this thy gracious will to us-ward!

5.

Stablished to fill the juice with vital vigour, giver of wealth, guard of his servant's body,
The great Priest, born, who knows the clouds, abider with men, is seated in the waters' eddy.

6.

Let the song, honouring the best, with longing honour the Asura's most famous sovran,
The deeds of him the mighty, deeds like Indra's, the manly one in whom the folk must triumph!

7.

In the two kindling-blocks lies Jatavedas like the well-cherished germ in pregnant women,--
Agni who day by day must be entreated by men who watch provided with oblations.

DECADE IV - AGNI

1.

Bring us most mighty splendour thou,
Agni, resistless on thy way:
Prepare for us the path that leads to glorious
opulence and strength!

2.

May the brave man, if full of zeal he serve and
kindle Agni's flame,
Duly presenting sacred gifts,
enjoy the Gods' protecting help.

3.

Thy bright smoke lifts itself aloft,
and far-extended shines in heaven,
For, Purifier! like the Sun thou beamest
with thy radiant glow.

4.

Thou, Agni, even as Mitra,
hast a princely glory of thine own.
Bright, active God, thou makest
fame increase like means of nourishment.

5.

At dawn let Agni, much-beloved,
guest of the house, be glorified,
In whom, the everlasting one,
all mortals make their offerings blaze.

6.

Most moving song be Agni's:
shine on high, O rich in radiant light!
Like the chief consort of a King riches and strength
proceed from thee.

7.

Exerting all our strength with thoughts of power
we glorify in speech
Agni your dear familiar friend,
the darling guest in every house.

8.

His beam hath lofty power of life:
sing praise to Agni, to the God
Whom men have set in foremost place,
like Mitra for their eulogy!

9.

To noblest Agni, friend of man,
chief Vritra-slayer, have we come-
Who with Srutarvan, Riksha's son,
in lofty presence is inflamed.

10.

Born as the loftiest Law commands, comrade of
those who grew with him.
Agni, the sire of Kasyapa by faith, the mother,
Manu, Sage.

DECADE V - AGNI

1.

We in King Soma place our trust,
in Agni, and in Varuna,
The Aditya, Vishnu, Surya,
and the Brahman-priest Brihaspati.

2.

Hence have these men gone up on high and
mounted to the heights of heaven:
On! conquer on the path by which Angirasas
travelled to the skies!

3.

That thou mayst send us ample wealth,
O Agni, we will kindler thee:
So, for the great oblation,
Steer, pray Heaven and Earth to come to us!

4.

He runs when one calls after him,
This is the prayer of him who prays.
He holds all knowledge in his grasp even as the felly
rounds the wheel.

5.

Shoot forth, O Agni, with thy flame:
demolish them on every side!
Break down the Yatudhana's strength,
the vigour of the Rakshasa!

6.

Worship the Vasus, Agni!
Here, the Rudras and Adityas, all
Who know fair sacrifices, sprung from Mann,
scattering blessings down!

BOOK II
CHAPTER I
DECADE I - AGNI

1.

Agni, thy faithful servant I call upon thee
with many a gift,
As in the keeping of the great inciting God.

2.

To Agni, to the Hotar-priest offer your best,
your lofty speech,
To him ordainer-like who bears the light of songs.

3.

O Agni, thou who art the lord of wealth in kine,
thou Son of Strength,
Bestow on us, O Jatavedas, high renown

4.

Most skilled in sacrifice, bring the Gods,
O Agni, to the pious, man:
A joyful Priest, thy splendour drives our foes afar

5.

Taught by seven mothers at his birth was he,
for glory of the wise.
He, firm and sure, hath set his mind
on glorious wealth

6.

And in the day our prayer is this:
May Aditi come nigh to help,
With loving-kindness bring us weal
and chase our foes

7.

Worship thou Jatavedas,
pray to him who willingly accepts,
Whose smoke wanders at will,
and none may grasp his flame

8.

No mortal man can e'er prevail by arts
of magic over him
Who hath served Agni well,
the oblation-giving God.

9.

Agni, drive thou the wicked foe,
the evil-hearted thief away,
Far, far, Lord of the brave! and give us easy paths!

10.

O hero Agni, Lord of men, on hearing this
new laud of mine
Burn down the Rakshasas, enchanters,
with thy flame!

DECADE II - AGNI

1.

Sing forth to him the holy, most munificent,
sublime with his refulgent glow,
To Agni, ye Upastutas

2.

Agni, he conquers by thine aid that brings him store
of valiant sons and does great deeds,
Whose bond of friendship is thy choice

3.

Sing praise to him the Lord of light! The Gods have
made the God to be their messenger,
To bear oblation to the Gods.

4.

Anger not him who is our guest! He is the bright
God Agni, praised by many a man,
God Hotar, skilled in sacrifice.

5.

May Agni, worshipped, bring us bliss: may the gift,
blessed one! and sacrifice bring bliss.
Yea, may our eulogies bring bliss.

6.

Thee have we chosen skilfullest in sacrifice,
immortal Priest among the Gods,
Wise finisher of this holy rite.

7.

Bring us that splendour, Agni, which may overcome
each greedy fiend in our abode,
And the malicious wrath of men!

8.

Soon as the eager Lord of men is friendly
unto Manu's race
Agni averteth from us all the Rakshasas!

DECADE III - INDRA

1.

Sing this, beside the flowing juice,
to him your hero, much-invoked,
To please him as a mighty Bull

2.

O Satakratu Indra, now rejoice with that
carouse of thine
Which is most glorious of all!

3.

Ye cows, protect the fount: the two mighty ones
bless the sacrifice.
The handles twain are wrought of gold.

4.

Sing praises that the horse may come; sing,
Srutakaksha, that the cow
May come, that Indra's might may come

5.

We make this Indra very strong to strike,
the mighty Vritra dead:
A vigorous hero shall he be.

6.

Based upon strength and victory and power,
O Indra, is thy birth:
Thou, mighty one! art strong indeed,

7.

The sacrifice made Indra great when he unrolled
the earth, and made
Himself a diadem in heaven.

8.

If I, O Indra, were, like thee,
the single ruler over wealth
My worshipper should be rich in kine.

9.

Pressers, blend Soma juice for him,
each draught most excellent, for him
The brave, the hero, for his joy.

10.

Here is the Soma juice expressed.
O Vasu, drink till thou art full:
Undaunted God, we give it thee.

DECADE IV - INDRA

1.

Surya, thou mountest up to meet the hero
famous for his wealth,
Who hurls the bolt and works for man.

2.

Whatever, Vritra-slayer! thou,
Surya hast risen upon to-day,
That, Indra, all is in thy power.

3.

That Indra is our youthful friend,
who with his trusty guidanceled
Turvasa, Yadu from afar.

4.

O Indra, let not ill designs surround us
in the sunbeams' light
This may we gain with thee for friend!

5.

Indra, bring wealth that gives delight,
the victor's ever-conquering wealth,
Most excellent, to be our aid

6.

In mighty battle we invoke Indra,
Indra is lesser fight,
The friend who bends his bolt at fiends.

7.

In battle of a thousand arms Indra drank
Kadru's Soma juice
There he displayed his manly might.

8.

Faithful to thee, we sing aloud,
heroic Indra, songs to thee
Mark, O good Lord, this act of ours!

9.

Hitherward! they who light the flame and
straightway trim the sacred grass,
Whose friend is Indra ever young.

10.

Drive all our enemies away,
smite down the foes who press around,
And bring the wealth for which we long!

DECADE V - INDRA AND OTHERS

1.

I Hear, as though 'twere close at hand,
the cracking of the whips they hold:
They gather splendour on their way.

2.

Indra, these friends of ours, supplied with Soma,
wait and look to thee
As men with fodder to the herd.

3.

Before his hot displeasure all the peoples,
all the men bow down,
As rivers bow them to the sea.

4.

We choose unto ourselves that high protection
of the mighty Gods,
That it may help and succour us.

5.

O Brahmanaspati, make thou
Kakshivan Ausija a loud
Chanter of flowing Soma juice!

6.

Much honoured with libations may the Vritra-slayer
watch for us:
May Sakra listen to our prayer

7.

Send us this day, God Savitar,
prosperity with progeny
Drive thou the evil dream away!

8.

Where is that ever-youthful Steer,
strong-necked and never yet bent down?
What Brahman ministers to him?

9.

There where the mountains downward slope,
there at the meeting of the streams
The Sage was manifest by song.

10.

Praise Indra whom our songs must laud,
sole sovran of mankind, the chief
Most liberal who controlleth men.

CHAPTER II
DECADE I - INDRA AND OTHERS

1.

Indra whose jaws are strong hath drunk of worshipping Sudaksha's draught,
The Soma juice with barley brew.

2.

O Lord of ample wealth, these songs of praise have called aloud to thee,
Like milch-kine lowing to their calves!

3.

Then straight they recognized the mystic name of the creative Steer,
There in the mansion of the Moon.

4.

When Indra, strongest hero, brought the streams, the mighty waters down,
Pushan was standing by his side.

5.

The Cow, the streaming mother of the liberal
Maruts, pours her milk,
Harnessed to draw their chariots on.

6.

Come, Lord of rapturous joys,
to our libation with thy bay steeds, come
With bay steeds to the flowing juice

7.

Presented strengthening gifts have sent
Indra away at sacrifice,
With night, unto the cleansing bath.

8.

I from my Father have received deep knowledge
of eternal Law:
I was born like unto the Sun.

9.

With Indra splendid feasts be ours, rich in all
strengthening things, wherewith,
Wealthy in food, we may rejoice

10.

Soma and Pushan, kind to him who travels
to the Gods, provide
Dwellings all happy and secure.

DECADE II - INDRA

1.

Invite ye Indra with a song to drink
your draught of Soma steeds, juice,
All-conquering Satakratu, most munificent of
all who live.

2.

Sing ye a song, to make him glad, to Indra,
Lord of tawny
The Soma-drinker, O my friends!

3.

This, even this, O Indra, we implore:
as thy devoted friends
The Kanvas praise thee with their hymns!

4.

For Indra, lover of carouse,
loud be our songs about the juice
Let poets sing the song of praise.

5.

Here, Indra, is thy Soma draught,
made pure upon the sacred grass:
Run hither, come and drink thereof

6.

As a good cow to him who milks,
we call the doer of good deeds
To our assistance duy by day.

7.

Hero, the Soma being shed,
I pour the juice for thee to drink
Sate thee and finish thy carouse!

8.

The Soma, Indra, which is shed in saucers
and in cups for thee,
Drink thou, for thou art lord thereof!

9.

In every need, in every fray we call,
as friends, to succour us,
Indra, the mightiest of all.

10.

O come ye hither, sit ye down:
to Indra sing ye forth your song,
Companions, bringing hymns of praise.

DECADE III - INDRA

1.

So, Lord of affluent gifts, this juice hath been
expressed for thee with strength:
Drink of it, thou who lovest song!

2.

Great is our Indra from of old;
greatness be his, the Thunderer
Wide as the heaven extends his might.

3.

Indra, as one with mighty arm,
gather for us with thy right hand
Manifold and nutritious spoil!

4.

Praise, even as he is known,
with song Indra the guardian of the kine,
The Son of Truth, Lord of the brave.

5.

With what help will he come to us,
wonderful, ever-waxing friend?
With what most mighty company?

6.

Thou speedest down to succour us this
ever-conquering God of yours
Him who is drawn to all our songs.

7.

To the assembly's wondrous Lord,
the lovely friend of Indra,
I Had prayed for wisdom and successs.

8.

May all thy paths beneath the sky whereby
thou speddest Vyasva on,
Yea, let all spaces hear our voice

9.

Bring to us all things excellent,
O Satakratu, food and strength,
For, Indra, thou art kind to us!

10.

Here is the Soma ready pressed:
of this the Maruts, yea, of this,
Self-luminous the Asvins drink.

DECADE IV - INDRA AND OTHERS

1.

Tossing about, the active ones came nigh to Indra at his birth,
Winning themselves heroic might.

2.

Never, O Gods, do we offend,
nor are we ever obstinate
We walk as holy texts command.

3.

Evening is come: sing loudly thou
Atharvan's nobly singing son:
Give praise to Savitar the God!

4.

Now Morning with her earliest light shines forth, dear daughter of the Sky:
High, Asvins, I extol your praise.

5.

Armed with the bones of dead Dadhyach,
Indra, with unresisted might
The nine-and-ninety Vritras slew.

6.

Come, Indra, and delight thee with the juice at all our Soma feasts,
Protector, mighty in thy strength

7.

O thou who slayest Vritras, come,
O Indra, hither to our side,
Mighty one, with thy mighty aids!

8.

That might of his shone brightly forth when Indra brought together, like
A skin, the worlds of heaven and earth,

9.

This is thine own Thou drawest near,
as turns a pigeon to his mate:
Thou carest, too, for this our prayer.

10.

May Vata breathe his balm on us, healthful,
delightful to our heart:
May he prolong our days of life.

DECADE V - INDRA AND OTHERS

1.

Ne'er is he injured whom the Gods
Varuna, Mitra, Aryam.
The excellently wise, protect.

2.

According to our wish for kine,
for steeds and chariots, as of old,
Be gracious to our wealthy chiefs

3.

Indra, these spotted cows yield thee
their butter and the milky draught,
Aiders, thereby, of sacrifice.

4.

That thou much-lauded! many-named!
Mayst, with this thought, that longs for milk,
Come to each Soma sacrifice.

5.

May bright Sarasvati, endowed with plenteous
wealth and spoil, enriched
With prayer, desire the sacrifice.

6.

Why 'mid the Nahusha tribes shall sate this Indra
with his Soma juice?
He shall bring precious things to us.

7.

Come, we have pressed the juice for thee;
O Indra, drink this Soma here:
Sit thou on this my sacred grass

8.

Great, unassailable must be the heavenly favour
of the Three,
Varuna, Mitra, Aryaman.

9.

We, Indra, Lord of ample wealth, our guide,
depend on one like thee,
Thou driver of the tawny steeds!

BOOK III
CHAPTER I
DECADE I - INDRA

1.

Let Soma juices make thee glad!
Display thy bounty, Thunderer:
Drive off the enemies of prayer!

2.

Drink our libation, Lord of hymns!
With streams of meath thou art bedewed:
Yea, Indra, glory is thy gift.

3.

Indra hath ever thought of you and
tended you with care.
The God, Heroic Indra, is not checked.

4.

Let the drops pass within thee as the rivers
flow into the sea
O Indra, naught excelleth thee!

5.

Indra, the singers with high praise,
Indra reciters with their lauds,
Indra the choirs have glorified.

6.

May Indra give, to aid us wealth handy
that rules the skilful ones!
Yea, may the Strong give potent wealth

7.

Verily Indra, conquering all,
drives even mighty fear away,
For firm is he and swift to act.

8.

These songs with every draught we pour come,
lover of the song, to thee
As milch-kine hasten to their calves.

9.

Indra and Wishan will we call for
friendship and prosperity,
And for the winning of the spoil.

10.

O Indra, Vritra-slayer, naught is better,
mightier than thou
Verily there is none like thee!

DECADE II - INDRA

1.

Him have I magnified, our Lord in common,
guardian of your folk,
Discloser of great wealth in kine.

2.

Songs have outpoured themselves to thee, Indra, the
strong, the guardian Lord,
And with one will have risen to thee!

3.

Good guidance hath the mortal man whom
Arya-man, the Marut host,
And Mitras, void of guile, protect.

4.

Bring us the wealth for which we long, O Indra,
that which is concealed
In strong firm place precipitous.

5.

Him your best Vritra-slayer, him the famous
champion of mankind
I urge to great munificence.

6.

Indra, may we adorn thy fame, fame of one like
thee, hero!
Deck, Sakra! Thy fame at highest feast!

7.

Indra, accept at break of day our Soma mixt
with roasted corn,
With groats, with cake, with eulogies!

8.

With waters' foam thou torest off, Indra,
the head of Namuchi,
When thou o'ercamest all the foes.

9.

Thine are these Soma juices, thine, Indra,
those still to be expressed:
Enjoy them, Lord of princely wealth!

10.

For thee, O Indra, Lord of light, Somas are pressed and grass is strewn:
Be gracious to thy worshippers!

DECADE III - INDRA

1.

We seeking strength, with Soma drops fill full your
Indra like a well,
Most liberal, Lord of boundless might.

2.

O Indra, even from that place come unto us with
food that gives
A hundred, yea, a thousand powers!

3.

The new-born Vritra-slayer asked his mother,
as he seized his shaft,
Who are the, fierce and famous ones?

4.

Let us call him to aid whose hands stretch far, the
highly-lauded, who
Fulfils the work to favour us

5.

Mitra who knoweth leadeth us,
and Varuna who guideth straight,
And Aryaman in accord with Gods.

6.

When, even as she were present here,
red Dawn hath shone from far away,
She spreadeth light on every side.

7.

Varuna, Mitra, sapient pair,
pour fatness on our pastures, pour
Meath on the regions of the air!

8.

And, at our sacrifices, these, sons, singers, have
enlarged their bounds,
So that the cows must walk knee-deep.

9.

Through all this world strode Vishnu: thrice his foot
he planted, and the whole
Was gathered in his footstep's dust.

DECADE IV - INDRA

1.

Pass by the wrathful offerer;
speed the man who pours libation, drink
The juice which he presents to thee!

2.

What is the word addressed to him,
God great and excellently wise?
For this is what exalteth him.

3.

His wealth who hath no store of kine hath ne'er
found out recited laud,
Nor song of praises that is sung.

4.

Lord of each thing that giveth strength,
Indra delighteth most in lauds,
Borne by bay steeds, libations' friend.

5.

With wealth to our libation come,
be not thou angry with us, like
A great man with a youthful bride.

6.

When, Vasu, wilt thou love the laud?
Now let the Channel bring the stream.
The juice is ready to ferment.

7.

After the Seasons. Indra, drink the Soma from the Brahman's gift:
Thy friendship is invincible!

8.

O Indra, lover of the song,
we are the singers of thy praise
O Soma-drinker, quicken us!

9.

O Indra, in each fight and fray give to our bodies manly strength:
Strong Lord, grant ever-conquering might!

10.

For so thou art the brave man's friend;
a hero, too, art thou, and strong:
So may thine heart be won to us!

DECADE V - Indra

1.

Like kine unmilked we call aloud, hero, to thee,
and sing thy praise,
Looker on heavenly light, Lord of this moving
world, Lord, Indra, of what moveth not!

2.

That we may win us wealth and power we poets,
verily, call on thee:
In war men call on thee, Indra, the hero's Lord,
in the steed's race-course call on thee:

3.

To you will I sing Indra's praise who gives good
gifts as well we know;
The praise of Maghavan who, rich in treasure, aids
his singers with wealth thousandfold.

4.

As cows low to their calves in stalls,
so with our songs we glorify
This Indra, even your wondrous God who checks
attack, who takes delight in precious juice.

5.

Loud singing at the sacred rite where Soma flows
we priests invoke
With haste, that he may help, as the bard's
cherisher, Indra who findeth wealth for you

6.

With Plenty for his true ally the active man will
gain the spoil.
Your Indra, much-invoked, I bend with song, as
bends a wright his wheel of solid wood.

7.

Drink, Indra, of the savoury juice, and cheer thee
with our milky draught!
Be, for our weal, our friend and sharer of the feast,
and let thy wisdom guard us well!

8.

For thou--come to the worshipper!--wilt find great
wealth to make us rich.
Fill thyself full, O Maghavan, for gain of kine, full,
Indra, for the gain of steeds!

9.

Vasishtha will not overlook the lowliest one among you all
Beside our Soma juice effused to-day let all the Maruts drink with eager haste!

10.

Glorify naught besides, O friends;
so shall no sorrow trouble you!
Praise only mighty Indra when the juice is shed,
and say your lauds repeatedly!

CHAPTER II
DECADE I - INDRA

1.

No one by deed attains to him who works and strengthens evermore:
No, not by sacrifice, to Indra. Praised of all, resistless, daring, bold in might.

2.

He without ligature, before making incision in the neck,
Closed up the wound again, most wealthy Maghavan, who healeth the dissevered parts.

3.

A thousand and a hundred steeds are harnessed to thy golden car:
Yoked by devotion, Indra, let the long-maned bays bring thee to drink the Soma juice!

4.

Come hither, Indra, with bay steeds, joyous,
with tails like peacock's plumes!
Let no men check thy course as fowlers stay the
bird: pass o'er them as o'er desert lands!

5.

Thou as a God, O mightiest,
verily blessest mortal man.
O Maghavan, there is no comforter but thou:
Indra, I speak my words to thee.

6.

O Indra, thou art far-renowned,
impetuous Lord of power and might.
Alone, the never-conquered guardian of mankind,
thou smitest down resistless foes.

7.

Indra for worship of the Gods,
Indra while sacrifice proceeds,
Indra, as warriors in the battle-shock, we call,
Indra that we may win the spoil.

8.

May these my songs of praise exalt thee, Lord, who
hast abundant wealth!
Men skilled in holy hymns, pure, with the hues of
fire, have sung them with their lauds to thee.

9.

These songs of ours exceeding sweet,
these hymns of praise ascend to thee,
Like ever-conquering chariots that display their
strength gain wealth and give unfailing help.

10.

Even as the wild-bull, when he thirsts,
goes to the desert's watery pool,
Come to us quickly both at morning and at eve, and
with the Kanvas drink thy fill!

DECADE II - INDRA AND OTHERS

1.

Indra, with all thy saving helps assist us,
Lord of power and might!
For after thee we follow even as glorious bliss, thee,
hero, finderout of wealth.

2.

O Indra, Lord of light, what joys thou broughtest
from the Asuras,
Prosper therewith, O Maghavan, him who lauds that
deed, and those whose grass is trimmed for thee!

3.

To Aryaman and Mitra sing a reverent song,
O pious one,
A pleasant hymn to Varuna who shelters us:
sing ye a laud unto the Kings!

4.

Men with their lauds are urging thee, Indra,
to drink the Soma first.
The Ribhus in accord have lifted up their voice, and
Rudras sung thee as the first.

5.

Sing to your lofty Indra, sing, Maruts,
a holy hymn of praise
Let Satakratu, Vritra-slayer, slay the foe with
hundred-knotted thunderbolt!

6.

To Indra sing the lofty hymn, Maruts!
That slays the Vritras best,
Whereby the holy ones created for the God the light
divine that ever wakes.

7.

O Indra, give us wisdom as a sire gives
wisdom to his sons
Guide us, O much-invoked, in this our way:
may we still live and look upon the light!

8.

O Indra, turn us not away:
be present with us at our feast
For thou art our protection, yea, thou art our kin:
O Indra, turn us not away!

9.

We compass these like waters, we whose grass is
trimmed and Soma pressed.
Here where the filter pours its stream,
thy worshippers round thee,
O Vritra-slayer, sit.

10.

All strength and valour that is found, Indra,
in tribes of Nahushas,
And all the splendid fame that the Five Tribes enjoy,
bring, yea, all manly powers at once!

DECADE III - INDRA

1.

Yea, verily thou art a Bull, our guardian,
rushing like a bull:
Thou, mighty one, art celebrated as a Bull,
famed as a Bull both near and far.

2.

Whether, O Sakra, thou be far, or,
Vritra-slayer, near at hand,
Thence by heaven-reaching songs he who bath
pressed the juice invites thee with thy long-maned
steeds.

3.

In the wild raptures of the juice sing to your hero
with high laud, to him the wise,
To Indra glorious in his name, the mighty one,
even as the hymn alloweth it!

4.

O Indra, give us for our weal a triple refuge,
triply strong!
Bestow a dwelling-place on our rich lords and me,
and keep thy dart afar from these!

5.

Turning, as 'twere, to meet the Sun enjoy from
Indra all good things!
When he who will be born is born with power we
look to treasures as our heritage.

6.

The godless mortal gaineth not this food,
O thou whose life is long!
But one who yokes the bright-hued horses, Etasas;
then Indra yokes his tawny steeds.

7.

Draw near unto our Indra who must be invoked
in every fight!
Come, thou most mighty Vritra-slayer, meet for
praise, come to, libations and to hymns!

8.

Thine, Indra, is the lowest wealth,
thou cherishest the midmost wealth,
Thou ever rulest all the highest: in the fray for cattle
none resisteth thee.

9.

Where art thou? Whither art thou gone? For many a place attracts thy mind.
Haste, warrior, fort-destroyer, Lord of battle's din! haste, holy songs have sounded forth!

10.

Here, verily, yesterday we let the thunder-wielder drink his fill.
Bring him the juice poured forth in sacrifice to-day. Now range you by the glorious one!

DECADE IV - INDRA

1.

He who as sovran Lord of men moves with his chariots unrestrained,
The Vritra-slayer, vanquisher of fighting hosts, pre-eminent, is praised in song.

2.

Indra, give us security from that whereof we are afraid
Help us, O Maghavan, let thy favour aid us thus; drive away foes and enemies!

3.

Strong pillar thou, Lord of the home! Armour of Soma-offerers!
The drop of Soma breaketh all the strongholds down, and Indra is the Rishis' friend.

4.

Verily, Surya, thou art great;
Truly, Aditya, thou art great!
O most admired for greatness of thy majesty, God,
by thy greatness thou art great!

5.

Indra! thy friend, when fair of form and rich in
chariots, steeds, and kine,
Hath ever vital power that gives him strength, and
joins the company with radiant men.

6.

O Indra, if a hundred heavens and if a hundred
earths were thine,--
No, not a hundred suns could match thee at thy
birth, not both the worlds, O Thunderer!

7.

Though, Indra, thou art called by men eastward and
west ward, north and south,
Thou chiefly art with Anava and Turvasa, brave
champion urged by men to come.

8.

Indra whose wealth is in thyself,
what mortal will attack this man?
The strong will win the spoil on the decisive day
through faith in thee, O Maghavan!

DECADE V - INDRA

1.

Call to your aid the eternal one who shoots and none
may shoot at him,
Inciter, swift, victorious, best of charioteers,
unconquered, Tugriya's strengthener!

2.

Let none, no, not thy worshippers,
delay thee far away from us
Even from faraway come thou unto our feast, or
listen if' already here!

3.

For Indra Soma-drinker, armed with thunder,
press the Soma juice;
Make ready your dressed meats: cause him to favour
us! The giver blesses him who gives.

4.

We call upon that Indra who, most active,
ever slays the foe
With boundless spirit, Lord of heroes, manliest one,
help thou and prosper us in fight!

5.

Ye rich in strength, through your great power
vouchsafe us blessings day and night!
The offerings which we bring to you shall never fail
gifts brought by us shall never fail.

6.

Whenever mortal worshipper will sing a bounteous
giver's praise,
Let him with song inspired laud Varuna who supports
the folk who follow varied rites.

BOOK IV
CHAPTER I
DECADE I - INDRA AND OTHERS

1.

These Soma juice mixt with curd have been expressed for Indra here:
Come with thy bay steeds, Thunder-wielder, to our home, to drink them till they make thee glad!

2.

Indra, these Somas with their lauds have been prepared for thy delight.
Drink of the pleasant juice and listen to our songs; lover of song, reward the hymn!

3.

I call on thee, Sabardugha, this day, inspirer of the psalm.
Indra, the richly-yielding milch-cow who provides unfailing food in ample stream.

4.

Indra, the strong and lofty hills
are powerless to bar thy way
None stays that act of thine when thou wouldst fain
give wealth to one like me who sings thy praise.

5.

Who knows what vital power he wins,
drinking beside the flowing juice?
This is the fair-cheeked. God who, joying in the
draught, breaks down the castles in his strength.

6.

What time thou castest from his seat and punishest
the riteless man,
Strengthen for opulence, O Indra Maghavan, our
plant desired by many a one!

7.

Let Tvashtar, Brahmanaspati, Parjanya guard our
heavenly word,
Aditi with her sons, the brothers, guard for us the
invincible, the saving word!

DECADE II

1.

Advancing, sending forth her rays,
the daughter of the Sky is seen.
The mighty one lays bare the darkness with her eye,
the friendly Lady makes the light.

2.

These morning sacrifices call you, Asvins,
at the break of day.
For help have I invoked you rich in power and might:
for, house by house, ye visit all.

3.

Where are ye, Gods? What mortal man, O Asvins,
glows with zeal for you,
Urging you with the crushing stone and with the stalk
of Soma thus or otherwise?

4.

This sweetest Soma juice hath been expressed for
you at morning rites.
Asvins, drink this prepared ere yesterday and give
treasures to him who offers it!

5.

Let me not, still beseeching thee with might and
sound of Soma drops,
Anger at sacrifice a fierce wild creature! Who would
not beseech the almighty one!

DECADE III

1.

Pressed is the juice divine with milk commingled: thereto hath Indra ever been accustomed. We wake thee, Lord of bays, with sacrifices: mark this our laud in the wild joys of Soma!

2.

A home is made for thee to dwell in, Indra: O much-invoked one, with the men go thither! Thou, that thou mayest guard us and increase us, givest us wealth and joyest in the Somas.

3.

The well thou clavest, settest free the fountains,and gavest rest to floods that were obstructed. Thou, Indra, laying the great mountain open, slaying the Ddnava, didst loose the torrents.

4.

When we have pressed the juice we laud thee,
Indra, most valorous! even about to win the booty.
Bring us prosperity, and by thy great wisdom, under
thine own protection, may we conquer!

5.

Thy right hand have we grasped in ours, O Indra,
longing, thou very Lord of wealth, for treasures.
Because we know thee, hero, Lord of cattle:
vouchsafe us mighty and resplendent riches!

6.

Men call on Indra in the armed encounter that he
may make the hymns they sing decisive.
Hero in combat and in love of glory, give us a
portion of the stall of cattle!

7.

Like birds of beauteous wing the Priyamedhas,
Rishis, imploring, have come nigh to Indra.
Dispel the darkness and fill full our vision: deliver us
as men whom snares entangle!

8.

They gaze on thee with longing in their spirit, as on a
strongwinged bird that mounteth sky-ward;
On thee with wings of gold, Varuna's envoy, the Bird
that hasteneth to the home of Yama.

9.

First in the ancient time was Prayer engendered:
Vena disclosed the bright ones from the summit,
Laid bare this world's lowest and highest regions,
womb of the existent and the non-existent.

10.

They have prepared and fashioned for this hero
words never matched, most plentiful,
most auspicious,
For him the ancient, great, strong, energetic, the
very mighty wielder of the thunder.

DECADE IV - INDRA

1.

The black drop sank in Ansumati's bosom,
advancing with ten thousand round about it.
Indra with might longed for it as it panted: the
hero-hearted King laid down his weapons.

2.

Flying in terror from the snort of Vritra all deities
who were thy friends forsook thee.
So, Indra, with the Maruts be thy friendship: in all
these battles thou shalt be the victor.

3.

The old hath waked the young Moon from his
slumber who runs his circling course
with many round him.
Behold the God's high wisdom in its greatness:
he who died yesterday to-day is living.

4.

Then, at thy birth, thou wast the foeman, Indra, of
those the seven who ne'er had met a rival.
The hidden pair, heaven and the earth, thou
foundest, and to the mighty worlds thou gavest
pleasure.

5.

A friend we count thee, sharp-edged,
thunder-wielder, Steer strong of body,
overthrowing many.
Thou, helping, causest pious tribes to conquer:
Indra, I laud the, heavenly Vritra-slayer.

6.

Bring to the wise, the great, who waxeth mighty
your offerings,. and make ready your devotion!
Go forth to many tribes as man's controller!

7.

Call we on Maghavan, auspicious Indra, best hero in
this fight where spoil is gathered,
Strong, listening to give us aid in battles, who slays
the Vritras, wins and gathers riches!

8.

Prayers have been offered up-through love of glory:
Vasishtha, honour Indra in the battle!

He who with fame extends through all existence
hears words which I, his faithful servant, utter.

9.

May the sweet Soma juices make him happy to cast
his quoit that lies in depth of waters!
Thou from the udder which o'er earth is fastened
hast poured the milk into the kine and herbage.

DECADE V - INDRA AND OTHERS

1.

This vigorous one whom deities commission, the conqueror of cars, the strong and mighty,
Swift, fleet to battle, with uninjured fellies, even Tarkshya for our weal will we call hither.

2.

Indra the rescuer, Indra the helper, hero who listens at each invocation,
Sakra I call, Indra invoked of many. May Indra Maghavan accept our presents!

3.

Indra whose right hand wields the bolt we worship, driver of bay steeds seeking sundered courses.
Shaking his beard with might he hath arisen, terrible with his weapons, with his bounty.

4.

The ever-slaying, bold and furious Indra, the bright bolt's Lord, the strong, the great, the boundless, Who slayeth Vritra and acquireth booty, giver of blessings, Maghavan the bounteous.

5.

The man who lies in wait and fights against us, deeming himself a giant or a hero,-- By battle or with strength destroy him, Indra! With thy help, manly-souled! may we be victors!

6.

He whom men call when striving with their foemen, or speeding onward in array of battle, Whom bards incite where heroes win the booty, or in the way to waters, He is Indra.

7.

On a high car, O Parvata and Indra, bring pleasant viands, with brave heroes, hither! Enjoy our presents, Gods, at sacrifices: wax strong by hymns, rejoice in our oblation!

CHAPTER II
DECADE I - INDRA

1.

The singers hymn thee, they who chant the psalm of praise are lauding thee.
The Brahmans have exalted thee,
O Satakratu, like a pole.

2.

All sacred-songs have magnified Indra expansive as the sea,
Best of all warriors borne on cars, the Lord of heroes, Lord of strength.

3.

This poured libation, Indra, drink, immortal, gladdening, excellent:
Streams of the bright have flowed to thee here at the seat of holy Law.

4.

Stone-darting Indra, wondrous God,
what wealth thou hast not given me here,
That bounty, treasure-finder!
Bring, filling full both thy hands, to us!

5.

O Indra, hear Tiraschi's call,
the call of him who serveth thee!
Satisfy him with wealth of kine and valiant
offspring! Great art thou.

6.

This Soma hath been pressed for thee,
O Indra: bold one, mightiest, come!
May Indra-vigour fill thee full,
as Surya fills mid-air with rays

7.

Come hither, Indra, with thy bays,
come thou to Kanva's eulogy!
Ye by command of yonder Dyaus, God bright by
day! have gone to heaven.

DECADE II - INDRA. DADHIKRAVAN

1.

ring forth oblations to the God who knoweth all who fain would drink,
The wanderer, lagging not behind the hero, coming nigh with speed!

2.

To us the mighty, lying in all vital power, who resteth in the deep, who standeth in the east.
Drive thou the awful word away.

3.

Even as a car to give us aid,
we draw thee nigh to favour us,
Strong in thy deeds, quelling attack, Indra, Lord, mightiest of the brave.

4.

With powers of mighty ones hath he, the friend,
the ancient, been equipped,
Through whom our father Manu made prayers
efficacious with the Gods.

5.

What time the swift and shining steeds,
yoked to the chariots, draw them on,
Drinking the sweet delightful juice, there men
perform their glorious acts.

6.

Him for your sake I glorify as Lord of Strength who
wrongeth none,
Indra the hero, mightiest, all-conquering and
omniscient.

7.

I with my praise have glorified strong Dadhikravan,
conquering steed
Sweet may he make our mouths:
may he prolong the days we have to live!

DECADE III - INDRA AND OTHERS

1.

Offer the triple sacred draught to Indu
hero-worshipper!
With hymn and plenty he invites you
to complete the sacrifice.

2.

Those whom they call the attendant pair of Kasyapa
who knows the light,
Lords of each holy duty when the wise have
honoured sacrifice.

3.

Sing, sing ye forth your songs of praise, men,
Priya-medhas, sing your songs:
Yea, let young children sing their lauds: yea, glorify
our firm stronghold!

4.

To Indra must a laud be said,
a joy to him who freely gives,
That Sakra may be joyful in our friendship
and the juice we pour.

5.

Your Lord of might that ne'er hath bent,
that ruleth over all mankind,
I call, that he, as he is wont, may aid the chariots
and the men.

6.

Even he who is thine own, through thought of
Heaven, of mortal man who toils,
He with the help of lofty Dyaus comes safe through
straits of enmity.

7.

Wide, Indra Satakratu,
spreads the bounty of thine ample grace:
So, good and liberal giver, known to all men,
send us splendid wealth!

DECADE IV - INDRA

1.

Heroes of one accord brought forth and
formed for kingship Indra who wins the
victory in all encounters,
For power, in firmness, in the field, the great
destroyer, and full of vigour.

2.

I trust in thy first wrathful deed, O Indra, when thou
slewest Vritra and didst work to profit man;
When the two world-halves fled for refuge unto thee,
and earth even trembled at thy strength,
O Thunder-armed!

3.

Come all with might together to the Lord of heaven,
the only one who is indeed the guestof men.
He is the first: to him who fain would come to us all
pathways turn; he is in truth the only one.

4.

Thine, Indra, praised of many, excellently rich, are we who trusting in thy help draw near to thee. For none but thou, song-lover, shall receive our lauds: as Earth loves all her creatures, welcome this our hymn!

5.

High hymns have sounded forth the praise of Maghavan, supporter of mankind, of Indra meet for lauds; Him who hath waxen mighty, much-invoked with prayers, immortal one whose praise each day is sung aloud.

6.

In perfect unison have all your longing hymns that find the light of heaven sounded forth Indra's praise. As wives embrace their lord, the comely bridegroom, so they compass Maghavan about that he may help.

7.

Make glad with songs that Ram whom many men invoke, worthy hymns of praise, Indra the sea of wealth; Whose boons spread like the heavens, the - lover of mankind: sing praise to him the Sage, most liberal for our good!

8.

I glorify that Ram who finds the light of heaven,
whose hundred strong and mighty ones
go forth with him.
With prayers may I turn hither Indra to mine aid;
the car which like a swift steed hasteth to the call!

PART SECOND
BOOK I
CHAPTER I

Om. Glory to the Samaveda! To Lord Ganesa glory!
Om.

I - Soma Pavamana

1.

Sing forth to Indu, O ye men,
to him who now is purified,
Fain to pay worship to the Gods!

2,

Together with thy pleasant juice
the Atharvans have commingled.
Divine, God-loving, for the God.

3.

Bring health to cattle with thy flow, health to the
people, health, to steeds,
Health, O thou King, to growing plants!

II - Soma Pavamana

1.

Bright are these Somas blent with milk,
with light that flashes brilliantly,
And form that shouteth all around.

2.

Roused by his drivers and sent forth, the strong
Steed hath come: nigh for spoil,
As warriors when they stand arrayed.

3.

Specially, Soma, Sage, by day,
coming together for our weal,
Like Surya, flow for us to see!

III - Soma Pavamana

1.

The streams of Pavamana, thine, Sage, mighty one,
have poured them forth,
Like coursers eager for renown.

2.

They have been poured upon the Reece towards the
meath-distilling vat:
The holy songs have rung aloud.

3.

Like milch-kine coming home, the drops of Soma
juice have reached the lake,
Have reached the shrine of sacrifice

IV - Agni

1.

Come, Agni, praised with song to feast and
sacrificial offerings:
sit As Hotar on the holy grass!

2.

So, Angiras, we make thee strong with
fuel and with holy oil.
Blaze high, thou youngest of the Gods!

3.

For us thou winnest, Agni, God, heroic strength
exceeding great, Far-spreading and of high renown.

V - Mitra Varuna

1.

Varuna, Mitra, sapient pair, pour fatness
on our pastures, pour
Meath on the regions of the air!

2.

Gladdened by homage, ruling far,
ye reign by majesty of might,
Pure in your ways, for evermore.

3.

Lauded by Jamadagni's song,
sit in the shrine of sacrifice:
Drink Soma, ye who strengthen Law!

VI - Indra

1.

Come, we have pressed theJuice for thee;
O Indra, drink this Soma here:
Sit thou on this my sacred grass!

2.

O Indra, let thy long-maned bays,
yoked by prayer, bring thee hitherward!
Give ear and listen to our prayers!

3.

We Soma-bearing Brahmans call thee
Soma-drinker with thy friend,
We, Indra, bringing Soma juice.

VII - Indra Agni

1.

Indra and Agni, moved by songs,
come to the juice, the precious dew:
Drink ye thereof, impelled by prayer!

2.

Indra and Agni, with the man who lauds
comes visible sacrifice:
So drink ye both this flowing juice!

3.

With force of sacrifice I seek Indra,
Agni who love the wise:
With Soma let them sate them here!

VIII - Soma Pavamana

1.

High is thy juice's birth: though set in heaven,
on earth it hath obtained
Dread sheltering power and great renown.

2.

Finder of room and freedom, flow for Indra
whom we must adore,
For Varuna and the Marut host!

3.

Striving to win, with him we gain all riches
from the enemy,
Yea, all the glories of mankind,

IX - Soma Pavamana

1.

Cleansing thee, Soma, in thy stream,
thou flowest in watery robe.
Giver of wealth, thou sittest in the place of Law, O
God, a fountain made of gold.

2.

He, milking for dear meath the heavenly udder, hath
sat in the ancient gathering-place.
Washed by the men, far-sighted, strong, thou
streamest to ther honourable reservoir.

X - Soma Pavamana

1.

Run onward to the reservoir and seat thee: cleansed
by the men speed forward to the battle.
Making thee glossy like an able courser, forth to
the sacred grass with reins they lead thee.

2.

Indu, the well-armed God is flowing onward, he
who averts the curse and guards the homesteads.
Father, begetter of the Gods, most skilful,
the buttress of the heavens and earth's supporter.

XI - Indra

1.

Like kine unmilked we call aloud, hero,
to thee, and sing thy praise,
Looker on heavenly light, Lord of this moving
world, Lord, Indra! Of what moveth not.

XII - Indra

1. With what help will he come to us,
wonderful, everwaxing friend?
With what most mighty company?

2.

What genuine and most liberal draught will spirit
thee with juice to burst
Open e'en strongly-guarded wealth?

CHAPTER II

I - INDRA

I.

Invite ye Indra with a song to drink
your draught of Soma juice.
All-conquering Satakratu,
most munificent of all who live!

2.

Lauded by many, much-invoked,
leader of song renowned of old:
His name is Indra, tell it forth!

3.

Indra, the dancer, be to us
the giver of abundant wealth:
The mighty bring it us knee-deep!

II - Indra

1.

Sing ye a song, to make him glad,
to Indra, Lord of tawny steeds,
The Soma-drinker, O my friends!

2.

To him, the bounteous, say the laud,
and let us glorify, as men
May do, the giver of true gifts!

3.

O Indra, Lord of boundless might,
for us thou seekest spoil and kine,
Thou seekest gold for us, good Lord!

III - Indra

1.

This, even this, O Indra,
we implore: as thy devoted friends,
The Kanvas praise thee with their hymns.

2.

Naught else, O Thunderer,
have I praised in the skilled singer's eulogy;
On thy laud only have I thought.

3.

The Gods seek him who presses out the Soma;
they desire not sleep:
They punish sloth unweariedly

ATHARVA VEDA

BOOK 1

HYMN I

A prayer to Vāchaspati for divine illumination and help.

1.

Now may Vāchaspati assign to me the strength and powers of those
Who, wearing every shape and form, the triple seven, are wandering round.

2.

Come thou again, Vāchaspati, come with divine intelligence.
Vasoshpati, repose thou here. In me be Knowledge, yea, in me.

3.

Here, even here, spread sheltering arms like
the two bow-ends strained with cord.
This let Vāchaspati confirm. In me be
Knowledge, yea, in me.

4.

Vāchaspati hath been invoked:
may he invite us in reply.
May we adhere to Sacred Lore.
Never may I be reft thereof.

HYMN II

A charm against dysentery

1.

We know the father of the shaft,
Parjanya, liberal nourisher,
Know well his mother: Prithivī,
Earth with her manifold designs.

2.

Do thou, O Bowstring, bend thyself around us:
make my body stone.

Firm in thy strength drive far away malignities
and hateful things.

3.

When, closely clinging round the wood,
the bowstring sings triumph to the swift and
whizzing arrow,
Indra, ward off from us the shaft, the missile.

4.

As in its flight the arrow's point hangs
between earth and firmament,
So stand this Munja grass between ailment
and dysenteric ill!

HYMN III

A charm against constipation and suppression
of urine

1.

We know the father of the shaft, Parjany
strong with hundred powers: By this may I
bring health unto thy body: Let the channels
pour their burthen freely as of old.

2.

We know the father of the shaft,
Mitra, the Lord of hundred powers:
By this, etc.

3.

We know the father of the shaft,
Varuna, strong with hundred powers:
By this, etc.

4.

We know the father of the shaft,
the Moon endowed with hundred powers:
By this, etc.

5.

We know the father of the shaft,
the Sun endowed with hundred powers:
By this may I bring health unto thy body:
let the channels pour their burthen
freely as of old.

6.

Whate'er hath gathered, as it flowed, in
bowels, bladder, or in groins,
Thus let the conduit, free from check, pour all
its burthen as of old.

7.

I lay the passage open as one cleaves the dam
that bars the lake:
Thus let, etc.

8.

Now hath the portal been unclosed as,
of the sea that holds the flood:
Thus let, etc.

9.

Even as the arrow flies away when loosened
from the archer's bow,
Thus let the burthen be discharged from
channels that are checked no more.

HYMN IV

To the waters, for the prosperity of cattle

1.

Along their paths the Mothers go, sisters of
priestly ministrants,
Blending their water with the mead.

2.

May yonder Waters near the Sun, or those
wherewith the Sun is joined,
Send forth this sacrifice of ours.

3.

I call the Waters, Goddesses, hitherward
where our cattle drink:
The streams must share the sacrifice.

4.

Amrit is in the Waters, in the Waters balm.
Yea, through our praises of the Floods,
O horses, be ye fleet and
strong, and, O ye kine, be full of strength.

HYMN V

To the waters, for strength and power

1.

Ye, Waters, truly bring us bliss:
so help us to strength and power
That we may look on great delight.

2.

Here grant to us a share of dew,
that most auspicious dew of yours,
Like mothers in their longing love.

3.

For you we fain would go to him to whose
abode ye send us forth,
And, Waters, give us procreant strength.

4.

I pray the Floods to send us balm, those who
bear rule o'er precious things,
And have supreme control of men.

HYMN VI

To the waters, for health and wealth

1.

The Waters be to us for drink, Goddesses,
for our aid and bliss:
Let them stream health and wealth to us.

2.

Within the Waters—Soma thus hath told me—
dwell all balms that heal,
And Agni, he who blesseth all.

3.

O Waters, teem with medicine to keep my
body safe from harm,
So that I long may see the Sun.

4.

The Waters bless us, all that rise in desert
lands or marshy pools!

Bless us the Waters dug from earth,
bless us the Waters brought
in jars, bless us the Waters of the Rains!

HYMN VII

To Indra and Agni, for the detection and destruction of evil spirits

1.

Bring the Kimidin hither,
bring the Yātudhāna self-declared
For Agni, God, thou, lauded, hast become the
Dasyu's slaughterer.

2.

O Jātavedas, Lord Supreme,
controller of our bodies, taste
The butter, Agni, taste the oil:
make thou the Yātudhānas mourn.

3.

Let Yātudhānas mourn, let all greedy
Kimidins weep and wail:
And, Agni, Indra, may ye both accept this
sacrifice of ours.

4.

May Agni seize upon them first, may
strong-armed Indra drive them forth:
Let every wicked sorcerer come hither and
say, Here am I.

5.

Let us behold thy strength, O Jātavedas.
Viewer of men, tell us the Yātudhānas.
Burnt by thy heat and making declaration
let all approach this sacrifice before thee.

6.

O Jātavedas, seize, on them:
for our advantage art thou born:
Agni, be thou our messenger
and make the Yātudhānas wail.

7.

O Agni, bring thou hitherward the Yātudhānas
bound and chained.
And afterward let Indra tear their heads off
with his thunderbolt.

HYMN VIII

To Indra, Brihaspati, Soma and Agni, for the destruction of sorcerers

1.

This sacrifice shall bring the Yātudhānas
as the flood brings foam:
Here let the doer of this deed woman or man,
acknowledge it.

2.

This one hath come confessing all:
do ye receive him eagerly.
Master him thou, Brihaspati;
Agni and Soma, pierce him through.

3.

O Soma-drinker, strike and bring the
Yātudhāna's progeny:
Make the confessing sinner's eyes fall from
his head, both right and left.

4.

As thou, O Agni Jātavedas, knowest the races
of these secret greedy beings,
So strengthened by the power of prayer,
O Agni, crushing them down
a hundred times destroy them.

HYMN IX

Benediction on a King at his inauguration

1.

May Indra, Pūshan, Varuria, Mitra, Agni,
benignant Gods, maintain this man in riches.
May the Ādityas and the Vive Devas
set and support him in supremest lustre.

2.

May light, O Gods, be under his dominion,
Agni, the Sun, all; that is bright and golden.
Prostrate beneath our feet his foes and rivals.
Uplift him to the loftiest cope of heaven.

3.

Through that most mighty prayer,
O Jātavedas, wherewith thou brought milk
to strengthen Indra,
Even therewith exalt this man, O Agni,
and give him highest rank among his kinsmen.

4.

I have assumed their sacrifice, O Agni, their
hopes, their glory, and their riches' fullness.
Prostrate beneath our feet his foes and rivals.
Uplift him to the loftiest cope of heaven.

HYMN X

Absolution of a sinner after intercession with
Varuna

1.

This Lord is the Gods' ruler; for the wishes of
Varuna the King must be accomplished.
Therefore, triumphant with the prayer I utter,
I rescue this man from the Fierce One's anger.

2.

Homage be paid, King Varuna, to thine anger;
for thou, dread God, detectest every falsehood.
I send a thousand others forth together:
let this thy servant live a hundred autumns.

3.

Whatever falsehood thou hast told,
much evil spoken with the tongue,
I liberate thee from the noose of Varuna
the righteous King.

4.

I free thee from Vaisvānara,
from the great surging flood of sin.
Call thou thy brothers, Awful One!
And pay attention to our prayer.

BOOK 2
HYMN I

Glorification of the prime cause of all things

1.

Vena beholds That Highest which lies hidden, wherein this all resumes one form and fashion. Thence Prisni milked all life that had existence: the hosts that know the light with songs extolled her.

2.

Knowing Eternity, may the Gandharva declare to us that highest secret station. Three steps thereof lie hidden in the darkness: he who knows these shall be the father's father.

3.

He is our kinsman, father, and begetter:
he knows all beings and all Ordinances.
He only gave the Gods their appellations:
all creatures go to him to ask direction.

4.

I have gone forth around the earth and heaven,
I have approached the first-born Son of Order.
He, putting voice, as 'twere, within the
speaker, stands in the world, he, verily is Agni.

5.

I round the circumjacent worlds have travelled
to see the far extended thread of Order.
Wherein the Gods, obtaining life eternal, have
risen upward to one common birthplace.

HYMN II

A charm to ensure success in gambling

1.

Lord of the World, divine Gandharva,
only he should be honoured

This is the cure for morbid flow,
this driveth malady away.

4.

The emmets from the water-flood produce
this healing medicine:
This is the cure for morbid flow,
this driveth malady away.

5.

Mighty is this wound-healing balm: from out
the earth was it produced.
This is the cure for morbid flow,
this driveth malady away.

6.

Bless us the Waters! Be the Plants auspicious!
May Indra's thunderbolt drive off the demons.
Far from us fall the shafts
they shoot against us!

HYMN IV

A charm to ensure health and prosperity by
wearing an amulet

1.

For length of life, for mighty joy,
uninjured, ever showing strength.
We wear Vishkandha's antidote,
the Amulet of Jangida.

2.

Amulet of a thousand powers,
Jangida save us, all around.
From Jambha, and from
Viara, Vishkandha, and tormenting pain.

3.

This overcomes Vishkandha,
this chases the greedy fiends away:
May this our panacea, may Jangida save us
from distress.

4.

With Jangida that brings delight,
Amulet given by the Gods,
We in the conflict overcome
Vishkandha and all Rākshasas.

5.

May Cannabis and Jangida preserve me from Vishkandha — that
Brought to us from the forest, this sprung from the saps of husbandry.

6.

This Amulet destroys the might of magic and malignity:
So may victorious Jangida prolong the years we have to live.

HYMN V

Invitation to, and praise of Indra

1.

Indra, be gracious, drive thou forth, come, Hero, with thy two bay steeds.
Taste the libation, hither, enjoying meath and the hymn, come, fair, to the banquet.

2.

O Indra, even as one athirst, fill thee with meath as 'twere from heaven.

Sweet-toned, the raptures of this juice have
come to thee as to the light.

3.

Swift-conquering Indra, Mitra like, smote,
as a Yati, Vritra dead.
Like Bhrigu he cleft Vala through,
and quelled his foes in Soma's rapturous joy.

4.

O Indra, let the juices enter thee. Fill full thy
belly, sate thee, mighty one!
Let the hymn bring thee.
Hear thou my call, accept the song I sing,
here, Indra, with thy friends enjoy thyself,
to height of rapture.

5.

Now will I tell the manly deeds of Indra,
the first that he achieved, the thunder-wielder.
He slew the Dragon, then disclosed the
waters, and cleft the channels
of the mountain torrents.

6.

He slew the Dragon lying on the mountain: his
heavenly bolt of thunder Tvashtar fashioned.
Like lowing kine in rapid flow descending the
waters glided downward to the ocean.

7.

Impetuous as a bull he chose the Soma,
and quaffed the juices in three sacred beakers.
Maghavan grasped the thunder for his
weapon, and smote to death this
first-born of the dragons.

BOOK 3
HYMN I

A prayer or charm for the defeat and destruction of enemies in battle

1.

Let the wise Agni go against our foemen,
burning against ill-will and imprecation
Let him bewilder our opponents' army,
Let Jātavedas smite and make them handless.

2.

Mighty are ye for such a deed, O Maruts.
Go forward, overcome them and destroy them.
The Vasus slew, and these were left imploring.
Wise Agni as our messenger assail them!

3.

O Maghavan, O Indra, thou who slayest
fiends, and, Agni, thou,

Burn, both of you, against these men,
the foeman's host that threatens us.

4.

Shot down the slope,
with thy two tawny coursers,
forth go thy bolt, destroying foes, O Indra!
Slay those who fly,
slay those who stand and follow.
On every side fulfil these men's intention.

5.

Indra, bewilder thou the foemen's army.
With Agni's, Vāta's furious rush drive them
away to every side.

6.

Let Indra daze their army.
Let the Maruts slay it with their might.
Let Agni take their eyes away,
and let the conquered host retreat.

HYMN II

A rifaccimento or recension of I

1.

May Agni, he who knows, our envoy, meet
them, burning against ill-will and imprecation.
May he bewilder our opponent's senses.
May Jātavedas smite and make them handless.

2.

This Agni hath bewildered all the senses
that were in your hearts:
Now let him blast you from your home,
blast you away from every side.

3.

Dazing their senses, Indra, come hitherward
with the wish and will.
With Agni's, Vāta's furious rush
drive them to every side away.

4.

Vanish, ye hopes and plans of theirs,
be ye confounded, all their thoughts!
Whatever wish is in their heart,
do thou expel it utterly.

5.

Bewildering the senses of our foemen, seize
on their bodies and depart, O Apvā!
Go meet them, flame within their hearts and
burn them. Smite thou the foes
with darkness and amazement.

6.

That army of our enemies, O Maruts, that
comes against us with its might, contending—
Meet ye and strike it with
unwelcome darkness so that not one of them
may know another.

HYMN III

A charm for the restoration of an expelled king

1.

Loudly he roared. Here let him labour deftly.
Spread, Agni, over spacious earth and heaven.
Let Maruts who possesses all treasures yoke
thee. Bring him who reverently paid oblations.

2.

Though he be far away, let the red
horses bring Indra, bring the sage to us and
friendship, Since with Sautrāmani Gods
for him o'erpower
Gāyatri, Brihatī, and hymn of praises.

3.

King Varuna call thee hither from the waters!
From hills and mountains
Soma call thee hither!
Let Indra call thee hither to these people.
Fly hither to these people as a falcon.

4.

May the hawk bring the man
who must be summoned, from far away,
in alien land, an exile.
May both the Asvins make thy pathway easy.
Come, and unite yourselves
with him, ye Kinsmen.

5.

Let thine opponents call thee back.
Thy friends have chosen, thee again.

Indra and Agni, all the Gods have kept
thy home amid the tribe.

6.

He who disputes our calling thee,
be he a stranger or akin.
Drive him, O Indra, far away,
and do thou bring this man to us.

HYMN IV

A benediction at the election of a king

1.

To thee hath come the kingship
with its splendour:
Shine as lord, sole ruler of the people.
King! let all regions of the heavens invite thee.
Here let men wait on thee and bow before
thee.

2.

The tribesmen shall elect thee
for the Kingship,
these five celestial regions shall elect thee.
Rest on the height and top of kingly power:
thence as a mighty man award us treasures.

3.

Kinsmen, inviting thee, shall go to meet thee,
with thee go Agni as an active herald.
Let women and their sons be friendly-minded.
Thou mighty one, shalt see abundant tribute.

4.

First shall the Asvins, Varuna and Mitra,
the Universal Gods, and Maruts call thee.
Then turn thy mind to giving gifts of treasures,
thence, mighty one,
distribute wealth among us.

5.

Speed to us hither from the farthest distance.
Propitious unto thee be Earth and Heaven.
Even so hath Varuna this King asserted,
he who himself hath called thee:
come thou hither.

6.

Pass to the tribes of men. O Indra, Indra.
Thou the Varunas hast been found accordant.
To his own place this one hath called thee,
saying, Let him adore the Gods and guide the
clansmen.

7.

The Bounteous Paths in sundry forms and
places, all in accord,
have given thee room and comfort.
Let all of these in concert call thee hither.
Live thy tenth decade here, a strong kind ruler.

HYMN V

A King's address to an amulet which is to strengthen his authority

1.

This Parna-Amulet hath come, strong and
destroying with its strength my rivals.
The power of the Gods,
the plants' sweet essence,
may it incite me ceaselessly with vigour.

2.

O Parna-Amulet, in me set firmly
might and opulence.
Within the compass of my rule may I be
rooted and supreme.

3.

That dear mysterious Amulet which
Gods have set within the tree,
May the Gods grant to me to wear together
with extended life.

4.

As Indra's gift, by Varuna instructed,
Parna hath come,
the mighty strength of Soma:
This would I, brightly shining,
love and cherish for long life
lasting through a hundred autumns.

5.

The Parna-Charm hath come to me
for great security from ill.
That I may be exalted, yea,
above the wealth of Aryaman.

6.

Sagacious builders of the car,
cleaver and skilful artisans,—
Make all the men on every side,
Parna, obedient to my will

7.

The kings and makers of the kings,
troop-leaders, masters of the horse,
Make all the men on every side, Parna,
obedient to my will.

8.

Thou, Parna, art my body's guard, man kin my birth to me a man.
With splendour of the circling year I bind thee on me, Amulet!

HYMN VI

Address to an amulet which is to secure the defeat of the wearer's enemies.

1.

Masculine springs from masculine,
Asvattha grows from Khadira,
May it destroy mine enemies,
who hate me and whom I detest.

2.

Crush down my foes, Asvattha!
Rend, O Burster, those who storm and rage,
With Indra, slayer of the fiends,
with Mitra and with Varuna.

3.

As thou hast rent and torn apart, Asvattha!
In the mighty sea,
So rend asundar all those men who hate me
and whom I detest.

4.

Thou who like some victorious bull displayest
thy surpassing might,
With thee, with thee, Asvattha!
We would overcome our enemies.

5.

Nirriti bind them with the bonds of Death
which never may be loosed.
Mine enemies, Asvattha!
Those who hate me and whom I detest.

6.

As thou, Asvastha!
Mountest on the trees and overthrowest them,
So do thou break my foeman's head asunder
and o'erpower him.

7.

Let them drift downward like a boat torn
from the rope that fastened it.
There is no turning back for those whom
He who Cleaves hath driven away.

8.

With mental power I drive them forth,
drive them with intellect and charm.
We banish and expel them with the branch
of an Asvattha tree.

HYMN VII

A charm with an amulet of buck horn to drive
away hereditary disease

1.

The fleet-foot Roebuck wears upon his head
a healing remedy.
Innate disease he drives away to all directions
with his horn.

2.

With his four feet the vigorous Buck hath
bounded in pursuit of thee.
Unbind the chronic sickness, Horn!
Deeply inwoven in the heart.

3.

That which shines younder, like a roof resting
on four walls, down on us,—
Therewith from out thy body
we drive all the chronic malady,

4.

May those twin stars, auspicious, named
Releasers, up in yonder sky.
Loose of the chronic malady
the uppermost and lowest bond.

5.

Water, indeed, hath power to heal,
Water drives malady away.
May water—for it healeth all—
free thee from permanent disease.

6.

Hath some prepared decoction brought
inveterate disease on thee,
I know the balm that healeth it:
we drive the malady away.

7.

What time the starlight disappears, what time
the gleams of dawn depart,
May evil fortune pass from us, the chronic
sickness disappear.

HYMN VIII

A charm to secure the submission, love, and
fidelity of kinsmen

1.

Let Mitra come, arranging, with the
Seasons, lulling the Earth to rest
with gleams of splendour.
And so let Agni, Varuna, and Vāyu make our
dominion tranquil and exalted.

2.

May Indra, Tvashtar hear my word with
favour, may Dhātar, Rāti, Savitar accept it.
I call the Goddess Aditi, heroes' mother,
that I may be the centre of my kinsmen.

3.

Soma I call, and Savitar with homage,
and all the Ādityas in the time of contest.
Long may this fire send forth its splendour,
lighted by kinsmen uttering no word against me.

4.

Here, verily, may you stay: go ye no farther.
The strong Herd,
Lord of Increase, drive you hither!
To please this man may all the Gods together
come unto you and be as dames who love him.

5.

We bend together all your minds, your vows
and purposes we bend.
We bend together you who stand apart with
hopes opposed to ours.

6.

I with my spirit seize and hold your spirits.
Follow with thought and
wish my thoughts and wishes.
I make your hearts the thralls of my dominion;
on me attendant come thy way I guide you.

HYMN IX

A charm against rheumatism (vishkondha)

1.

Heaven is the sire, the mother Earth,
of Karsapha and Visapha.
As ye have brought them hither, Gods!
So do ye move them hence away.

2.

The bands hold fast without a knot:
this is the way that Manu used.
I make Vishkandha impotent
as one emasculateth bulls.

3.

Then to a tawny-coloured string the wise
and skilful bind a brush.
Let bandages make impotent the strong
and active Kābava.

4.

Ye who move active in your strength like
Gods with Asuras' magic powers,
Even as the monkey scorns the dogs,
Bandages! Scorn the Kābava.

5.

Yea, I will chide thee to thy shame,
I will disgrace the Kābava.
Under our impracations ye,
like rapid cars, shall pass away.

6.

One and one hundred over earth are the
Vishkandhas spread abroad.
Before these have they fetched thee forth.
Vishkandha quelling Amulet.

HYMN X

A new year prayer

1.

The First hath dawned.
With Yama may it be a cow to pour forth milk.
May she be rich in milk and stream for us
through many a coming year.

2.

May she whom Gods accept with joy,
Night who approacheth as a cow,
She who is Consort of the Year,
bring us abundant happiness

3.

Thou whom with reverence we approach,
O Night, as model of the Year,
Us children long to live;
bless us with increase of our wealth.

4.

This same is she whose light first dawned
upon us: she moves established
in the midst of others:

Great powers and glories are contained within
her: a first-born bride,
she conquers and bears children.

5.

Loud was the wooden pass-gear's ring and
rattle, as it made annual oblation ready.
First Ashtakā! May we be lords of riches, with
goodly children and good men about us.

6.

The shrine of Ilā flows with oil and fatness:
accept, O Jātavedas, our oblations.
Tame animals of varied form and colour—
may all the seven abide with me contented.

7.

Come thou to nourish and make me prosper.
Night! May the favour of the Gods attend us.
Filled full, O Ladle, fly thou forth.
Completely filled fly back again.
Serving at every sacrifice bring to us
food and energy.

8.

This Year hath come to us,
thy lord and consort, O Ekāshtakā.
Vouchsafe us children long to live,
bless us with increase of our wealth.

9.

The Seasons, and the Seasons' Lords
I worship, annual parts and groups.
Half years, Years, Months, I offer to the Lord
of all existing things.

10.

I offer to the Seasons,
to their several groups, to Months, to Years.
Dhātar, Vidhātar, Fortune,
to the lord of all existing things.

11.

With fatness and libation we sacrifice
and adore the Gods.
Wealthy in kine may we retire to rest us
in our modest homes.

12.

Ekāshtakā, burning with zealous fervour,
brought forth her babe the great and glorious
Indra.
With him the Gods subdued their adversaries:
the Lord of Might became the Dasyus' slayer.

13.

Indra's and Soma's mother!
Thou art daughter of Prajāpati.
Satisfy thou our hearts' desires.
Gladly accept our sacrifice.

HYMN XI

A charm for the recovery of a dangerously
sick man

1.

For life I set thee free by this oblation
both from unmarked'.
Decline and from consumption:
Or if the grasping demon have possessed him,
free him from her, O Indra, thou and Agni!

2.

Be his days ended, be he now departed, be he
brought very near to death already,
Out of Destruction's lap again I bring him,
save him for life to last a hundred autumns.

3.

With sacrifice thousand-eyed and
hundred-powered, bringing a hundred lives,
have I restored him,
That Indra through the autumns may conduct
him safe to the farther shore of all misfortune.

4.

Live, waxing in thy strength a hundred
autumns, live through a hundred springs,
a hundred winters!
Indra, Agni, Savitar, Brihaspati
give thee a hundred! With hundred-lived
oblation have I saved him,

5.

Breath, Respiration, come to him,
as two car-oxen to their stall!
Let all the other deaths,
whereof men count a hundred, pass away.

6.

Breath, Respiration, stay ye here.
Go ye not hence away from him,
Bring, so that he may reach old age,
body and members back again.

7.

I give thee over to old age,
make thee the subject of old age.
Let kindly old age lead thee on.
Let all the other deaths,
whereof men count a hundred, pass away!

8.

Old age hath girt thee with its bonds
even as they bind a bull with rope.
The death held thee at thy birth
bound with a firmly-knotted noose,
Therefrom, with both the hands of Truth,
Brihaspati hath loosened thee.

BOOK 4
HYMN I

Cosmogonical and mystico-theological doctrine

1.

Eastward at first the prayer was generated:
Vena disclosed bright flashes from the summit,
Disclosed his deepest, nearest revelations,
womb of the non-existent and existent.

2.

Let this Queen come in front, her Father's daughter,
found in the worlds for earliest generation.
For him they set this radiant vault in motion.
Let them prepare warm milk
for him who first would drink.

3.

He who was born as his all-knowing kinsman
declareth all the deities' generations.
He from the midst of prayer his prayer hath taken.
On high, below, spread forth his godlike nature.

4.

For he, true to the law of Earth and Heaven,
established both the mighty worlds securely.
Mighty when born, he propped apart the mighty,
the sky, our earthly home, and air's mid-region.

5.

He from the depth hath been reborn for ever,
Brihaspati the world's sole Lord and Ruler.
From light was born the Day with all its lustre:
through this let sages live endowed with splendour.

6.

The sage and poet verily advanceth the statute
of that mighty God primeval.
He was born here with many more beside him:
they slumbered when the foremost side was opened.

7.

The man who seeks the friend of Gods,
Atharvan the father, and Brihaspati, with worship,
Crying to him, Be thou all things' creator!
The wise God, self-dependent, never injures.

Hymn II is missing

HYMN III

A Charm against tigers, wolves, thieves and other noxious creatures

1.

Three have gone hence and passed away,
the man, the tiger, and the wolf.
Down, verily, the rivers flow,
down-goeth the celestial tree.
Down let our foemen bend and bow.

2.

On distant pathway go the wolf,
on pathway most remote the thief!
On a far road speed forth the rope with teeth,
and the malicious man!

3.

We crush and rend to pieces both thine eyes, O Tiger,
and thy jaws and all the twenty claws we break.

4.

We break and rend the tiger first of creatures
that are armed with teeth;
The robber then, and then the snake,
the sorcerer, and then the wolf.

5.

The thief who cometh near to-day
departeth bruised and crushed to bits.
By nearest way let him be gone.
Let Indra slay him with his bolt.

6.

Let the beast's teeth be broken off,
shivered and shattered be his ribs!
Slack be thy bowstring:
downward go the wild beast that pursues the hare!

7.

Open not what thou hast compressed,
close not what thou hast not compressed.
Indra's and Soma's child,
thou art Atharvan's tiger-crushing charm.

BOOK 5

HYMN I

A glorification of Trita and Varuna

1.

He who with special plans and deathless spirit,
waxing, well-born, hath come unto his birth-place,
As he who shines upholds the days, thus Trita,
of pure life, bears the Three as their supporter.

2.

He who, the first, approached the holy statutes
makes, after, many beauteous forms and figures.
Eager to drink, his birth-place first he entered who
understands the word when yet unspoken.

3.

He who—the fluid gold, with radiant kinsmen—
to fervent glow delivered up thy body,
On him both set names, that shall live for ever:
to him the regions shall send robes to clothe him.

4.

As these have gone to their primeval station,
each gaining an imperishable dwelling,
May kissing mothers of the bards' beloved bring the
pole-drawing husband to the sister.

5.

By holy wisdom I a sage, Far-Strider!
Offer to thee this lofty adoration.
This worship both the mighty eddying rivers,
coming together to this station, heighten.

6.

Seven are the pathways which the wise have
fashioned: to one of these
may come the troubled mortal.
On sure ground where the ways are parted standeth
Life's Pillar in the dwelling of the Highest.

7.

Working, I go my way with deathless spirit:
life, spirit, bodies have gone gladly thither.
Aye, Sakra also gives his gift of treasure
as when the sacrifice meets with power.

8.

Yea, the son asks dominion of his father:
this they declared the noblest path to welfare.
Varuna, let them see thy revelations: display the
wondrous shapes of times to follow.

9.

Halt with the milk, its other half,
thou minglest and with that half, strong! Unbeguiled!
Let us exalt the gracious friend, the mighty,
Varuna son of Aditi, strength-giver.
We have told him the marvels sung by poets.
The utterance of Heaven and Earth is truthful.

HYMN II

A glorification of Indra

1.

In all the worlds that was the best and highest
whence sprang the Mighty One of splendid valour.
As soon as born he overcomes his foemen,
when those rejoice in him who bring him succour.

2.

Grown mighty in his strength, with ample vigour,
he as a foe strikes fear into the Dāsa,
Eager to win the breathing and the breathless:
All sang thy praise at banquet and oblation.

3.

All concentrate on thee their mental vigour what
time these, twice or thrice, are thine assistants,
Blend what is sweeter than the sweet with sweetness
win quickly with our meath that meath in battle.

4.

If verily in every war the sages
joy and exult in thee who win treasures,
With mightier power, strong God,
extend thy firmness:
let not malevolent Kaokas harm thee.

5.

Proudly we put our trust in thee in battles, when we
behold great wealth the prize of combat.
I with my words impel thy weapons onward, and
sharpen with my prayer thy vital vigour.

6.

Thou in that house, the highest or the lowest,
which thy protection guards, bestowest riches.
Establish ye the ever-wandering mother,
and bring full many deeds to their completion.

7.

Praise in the height Him who hath many pathways,
courageous, strongest, Aptya of the Aptyas.
Through strength he shows himself of ample power:
pattern of Prithivī, he fights and conquers.

8.

Brihaddiva, the foremost of light-winners, hath made
these holy prayers, this strength for Indra.
Free Lord, he rules the mighty fold of cattle,
winning, aglow, even all the billowy waters.

9.

Thus hath Brihaddiva, the great Atharvan,
spoken to Indra as himself in person.
Two sisters free from stain, the Mātarivans,
with power impel him onward and exalt him.

HYMN III

A prayer to Agni, Indra, and other deities for victory and prosperity

1.

Let strength be mine while I invoke thee, Agni!
Enkindling thee may we support our bodies.
May the four regions bend and bow before me:
with thee for guardian may we win the combat.

2.

Baffling the range of our opponents, Agni!
Guard us as our protector round about us.
Down the slope go they who hate us, backward,
and let their thought who watch at home be ruined.

3.

May all the Gods be on my side in battle,
the Maruts led by Indra, Vishnu, Agni.
Mine be the middle air's extended region,
and may the Wind blow favouring these my wishes.

4

For me let them present all mine oblations,
and let my mind's intention be accomplished.
May I be guiltless of the least transgression:
may all the Gods come hither and protect me.

5.

May the Gods grant me riches, may the blessing and invocation of the Gods assist me.
This boon shall the celestial Hotars win us:
may we, unwounded, have brave heroes round us.

6.

Ye six divine Expanses, give us freedom.
Here, all ye Gods, acquit yourselves like heroes.
Let not calamity or curse o'ertake us, nor deeds of wickedness that merit hatred.

7.

Do ye three Goddesses give ample shelter and all success to us ourselves and children.
Let us not lose our children or our bodies: let us not benefit the foe, King Soma!

8.

Foodful and much-invoked, at this our calling may the far-reaching Bull grant us wide shelter.
Lord of bay coursers, Indra, bless our children: harm us not, give us not as prey to others.

9.

Lord of the world, Creator and Disposer, may the
God Savitar who quells assailants,
May the Ādityas, Rudras, both the Asvins, Gods,
guard the sacrificer from destruction.

10.

Let those who are our foemen stay afar from us: with
Indra and with Agni we will drive them off.
The Ādityas and the Rudras, over us on high, have
made me strong, a thinker, and a sovran lord.

11.

Yea, we call Indra hitherward, the winner of wealth
in battle and of kine and horses.
May he mark this our worship when we call him,
Lord of bay steeds, thou art our friend and comrade.

BOOK 6
HYMN I

In praise of Savitar

1.

Sing, Atharvana, at eve, sing loudly, bring a splendid present: hymn God Savitar with praises.

2.

Yea, praise him whose home is in the river,
Son of Truth, the youthful,
gracious friend whose word is guileless.

3.

Savitar our God shall send us many everlasting treasures, that both paths may well be travelled.

HYMN II

In praise of Indra

1.

For Indra, ministering priests!
Run ye and press the Soma juice,
That he may hear his praiser's word,
and this my call.

2.

Thou into whom the drops find way
as sap pours life into a tree,
Drive off in thine abundant might our demon foes.

3.

For Indra, thunder-armed, who drinks the Soma press
the Soma out:
He, youthful, conqueror, and Lord is praised by all.

HYMN III

A prayer to various deities for protection and
prosperity

1.

Guard us the Maruts!
Guard us well, O Indra, Piishan, Aditi.
Guard us, O Waters' Child, and Rivers Seven.
May Vishnu guard us, and the Sky.

2.

May Heaven and Earth take care of us for victory,
may Pressing-Stone and Soma save us from distress.
Sarasvati, auspicious Goddess, guard us well:
preserve us Agni and his kind protecting powers.

3.

Preserve us both the Asvins,
Gods and Lords of Light,
and let the Dawns and Night bring us deliverance.
The Waters' Child protect our house
from every harm. Do thou,
God Tvashtar, make us strong for health and wealth.

HYMN IV

A hymn to various deities for protection

1.

May Tvashtar, Brāhmanaspati,
Parjanya hear my holy prayer.
May Aditi with all her sons, the brothers, guard us,
invincible, protecting power.

2.

May Ansa, Bhaga, Varuna, and Mitra, Aryaman,
Aditi, and Maruts guard us.
May we be freed from that oppressor's hatred. May
he keep off that foeman who is near us.

3.

May both the Asvins further our devotion.
With ceaseless care
deliver us, Wide-Ranger! O Father Heaven,
keep from us all misfortunes.

HYMN V

A prayer to Agni and Indra for the well-being of a
princely patron

1.

Agni, adored with sacred oil,
lift up this man to high estate.
Endow him with full store of strength and make him
rich in progeny.

2.

Advance him, Indra!
Let him be ruler of all akin to him.
Grant him sufficiency of wealth: guide him to life
and length of days.

3.

Prosper this man, O Agni,
in whose house we offer sacrifice.
May Soma bless him, and the God here present,
Brāhmanaspati.